Miracles Masters & Mirth

Adventures in Spirituality and Self-Awareness

Therese Emmanuel Grey

Copyright © 2009 Sirius Publishing Partners
All rights reserved
ISBN 978-0-9748616-3-0
Printed in the U.S.A

Cover art © 2009 Marius Michael George
www.mariusfineart.com
All rights reserved.

Dedication

*To my husband Brian,
for being willing to wrestle with my lesser self
and for teaching me how to love.*

Gnosis

The direct experiential knowledge of the supernatural or divine. This is not enlightenment understood in its general sense of insight or learning but enlightenment that validates the existence of the supernatural.

He Leadeth Me

He leadeth me, O blessed thought!
O words with heav'nly comfort fraught!
Whate'er I do, where'er I be
Still 'tis God's hand that leadeth me.
He leadeth me, He leadeth me,
By His own hand He leadeth me;
His faithful follower I would be,
For by His hand He leadeth me.
Sometimes mid scenes of deepest gloom,
Sometimes where Eden's bowers bloom,
By waters still, over troubled sea,
Still 'tis His hand that leadeth me.
Lord, I would place my hand in Thine,
Nor ever murmur nor repine;
Content, whatever lot I see,
Since 'tis my God that leadeth me.
And when my task on earth is done,
When by Thy grace the vict'ry's won,
E'en death's cold wave I will not flee,
Since God through Jordan leadeth me.

Joseph H. Gilmore, 1862
28-year-old Baptist minister

Gather us in

Gather us in, thou Love that fillest all
Gather our rival faiths within thy fold
Rend every temple-veil, and bid it fall,
That we may know that thou hast been of old.

Gather us in, we worship only thee.
In varied names we stretch a common hand.
In differing forms a common soul we see,
In many ships we seek one spirit-land.

Each sees one colour in thy rainbow light.
Each looks upon one tint and calls it heaven.
Thou art the fullness of our partial sight.
We are not perfect till we find the seven.

Some seek a Father in the heavens above.
Some ask a human image to adore.
Some crave a Spirit vast as life and love.
Within thy mansions we have all and more.

George Matheson, 1890
Blind Presbyterian poet

Table of Contents

Mitakuye Oyasin • 15
Be ye as a little child • 19
The valley of the shadow of death • 24
The sufis • 26
Saint Germain and the violet flame • 30
Presencia Yo Soy • 33
Love holds everything together • 35
Jewels in the heart • 38
A voice out of heaven • 39
By their fruits shall ye know them • 41
Staying in tune • 48
The gas chamber • 49
The burning coal • 52
Driving on empty • 53
Archangel Michael, help me! • 55
An angel in a pickup truck • 56
The yellow ray • 58
Blessing food • 60
Double rainbows • 61
Shiva! Shiva! Shiva! • 63

Focuses of light ♦ 69

A special clearance ♦ 71

The river ♦ 73

A perfect fit ♦ 75

The body of Christ ♦ 77

Holy Christ Self above me ♦ 79

Angel of the Presence ♦ 81

Violet flame blazing ♦ 83

Minuteman for Saint Germain ♦ 84

A "near death" experience ♦ 88

Auld Lang Syne ♦ 93

The servant leader ♦ 95

The gift of the Guru ♦ 98

Yellow bottles ♦ 99

O Christmas tree ♦ 100

Spiritual mantles ♦ 102

Messenger of Music ♦ 107

A marriage made in heaven ♦ 108

Reverse the tide ♦ 114

The second coming ♦ 116

The Promise ♦ 121

Mother Mary in a suit ♦ 123
The psychology of success ♦ 125
Saying goodbye ♦ 128
The Lost Chord ♦ 130
Parlez moi d'amour ♦ 132
Please come into my heart ♦ 134
Lanello ♦ 135
Love conquers fear ♦ 136
The labors of Hercules ♦ 139
The all-seeing eye of God ♦ 142
God is healing you now ♦ 144
The sponsoring master ♦ 146
Mercy's flame ♦ 148
Past lives ♦ 150
The Legend of the Ancient of Days ♦ 152
A song for our king ♦ 165
A third-eye blessing ♦ 167
A rose from heaven ♦ 168
Windows of opportunity ♦ 171
Holy water! ♦ 173
The blue chandelier ♦ 175

Come back, right away ♦ 176
Out-of-body experiences ♦ 178
A mountain of garbage ♦ 180
The great initiator♦ 182
Ancient mystic rites ♦ 184
A daily prayer ♦ 189
The presence actual   191
Do you hear the people sing? ♦ 193
A spiritual statement of purpose ♦ 199
Spiritual resources ♦ 202

Mitakuye Oyasin

Hi. My name is Therese Emmanuel Grey. I am the eldest of a family of seven and today, a mother of four. Our home is in Paradise Valley, Montana. Over the years, I lived many "lives." I have worked in all kinds of jobs, from internships in international business and public affairs to positions in communication and journalism, from waitressing and pizza delivering to camp counseling and personal coaching, and from teaching jobs for adults and children to raising a family and running a home business. Each of these cycles set the stage for the greatest pursuit of all, my search to find God.

When I was a young adult, I started to really question life. What was it all about? Why were we here? I knew there had to be a purpose. I believed in God, but I did not want to be confined to a particular religion. It seemed to me that God was big enough for all religious experiences. I started looking for the threads of consciousness that unite Christians, Buddhists, Hindus, Jews and Moslems, as well as the ancient Egyptians and Greeks. In so doing, I discovered mysticism.

I continued my quest for truth and the universe responded, powerfully, unequivocally, and compassionately. Still, there were many tests to pass, many trying times, and much soul searching. I came face-to-face with death, with my deepest fears, and with a lot of pain, both emotionally and physically.

Looking back on this leg of the journey, I was truly blessed. God never let go of me. Through darkest nights and brightest days, He was there, She was there. Now twenty years later, I have a story to tell.

This book is about some of the real, down-to-earth miracles that happened to me. Some were astounding, others more subtle. Each brought me closer to the great, ever-expanding, all-encompassing mystery of love that is God and that thrills my heart and soul.

My experiences are, in a sense, not unique. God speaks to each one of us in a very personal way, and every one I know who has tread the spiritual path also has stories to tell. Still, it is my hope that within these pages, you will find inspiration and a renewed sense of purpose that will accelerate your own path and soul awakening.

What is the soul? It is a spherical ovoid of light that enfolds our body as a childlike presence. The soul is separate from our personality and from the identity that we have come to know as "me" and "you." The soul is both familiar and elusive. It simply is.

Over the years, God has shown me specific past life records and karmas that my soul has gone through. I can see the learning opportunities that thread each of these lives together and rejoice in the understanding that I am all of these, and none of these, simultaneously.

My identity, like yours, is not limited to the roles played in the great drama of life. Neither is it limited to the roles that lie ahead. It resides beyond the veil of human consciousness and form, yet continues to press in, to merge with soul awareness. I am the observer, watching the process unfold, day by day, year by year, through the grace and patience of the hand of God.

Why am I here? Why are you here? To graduate from all of these lifetimes, to seal the lessons learned and to give back to life for the opportunity given. This process has been described as the ascension in the mystery schools of old, in the biblical records, as well as in the teachings of Theosophy.

Others have walked this path before me, and before you, and have graduated from these halls of learning, often referred to as a "school of hard knocks." At the close of earthly life, their consciousness ascended into higher octaves. The spiritual transformation that they experienced did not cancel out their identity. On the contrary, it crystallized all of the good, all of the love, all of the understanding, constancy, devotion and courage anchored through lifetimes on earth. They became ascended masters, immortals, beings of light with brilliant white auras.

The idea of ascended masters is not that "far out" a concept. Ascended masters are spiritual beings like us, who, as author and near-death survivor Dannion Brinkley explains, are evolving in the heaven-world instead of having a human experience. When Jesus went up on a mountain with his disciples Peter, James and John, the ascended masters Moses and Elijah appeared to him and interacted with him. This is recorded in the book of Matthew.

My husband Brian, who had a near-death experience as

a SIDS baby and two subsequent out-of-body (OBE) experiences when he was twenty-eight, remembers his encounters with the masters and the angels. I also heard another near-death survivor, Betty Eadie, author of *Embraced by the Light*, explain in an interview that when someone passes away, they are greeted by the master they feel most comfortable with, like Buddha for the Buddhists or Shiva for the Hindus. In her case, Jesus was the master who greeted her "upon arrival."

There are as many ascended masters as there are stars in heaven. Some specifically focus their attention and efforts on helping us in our human travails, limited nevertheless by our free will and our returning karma. In my search for God, I came into contact with them through deep striving and communion, as well as through the portals of spiritual initiation. These masters are my friends. I recognize their vibration as clearly as my own reflection when I look in the mirror.

I feel their closeness, their love, and their concern. On many occasions, they have interceded in my life in very real, tangible ways. The help, the comfort, the discipline, the correction they afforded me, they would also give you.

This is my story, our story, and your story, if you will let it unfold, for we are all, as the Lakota proclaim, related.

Mitakuye Oyasin.

Be ye as a little child

My first memories communing with God were as a little girl, growing up in France. I was born next to the Cathedral of the Sacred Heart in Paris, and learned to walk holding its gates. I remember playing in the sandboxes under its towering dome. I remember going into the basilica and looking at the large painting of Jesus on the ceiling. When people asked me what I wanted to be when I grew up, I told them I wanted to become a nun, which alarmed my grandfather, who wanted a more worldly occupation for me.

These early years were not unblemished and on several occasions, I directly experienced God's rescuing hand. Has it not been said that if it wasn't for heaven's intercession, we might never make it through childhood?

My mom tells me that when I was an infant, she left me in a stroller outside a post office building in Paris so she could quickly run in. It was 1970. Life was more laid back then, and my mom, who was still very young, didn't see any harm in it. As she came out of the building, she saw an older, suspicious-looking woman pushing the stroller away, and ran to save me. Looking back at this moment, I shudder to think of where I might be today if the kidnapping had been successful.

The next incident I clearly remember. We had just moved to Chantilly, a beautiful town twenty-five miles north of Paris. I was three years old. In the evenings, my parents often took my younger brother and I for long walks around Chantilly's world famous racetrack. One day, I fell behind them picking flowers in the grass. I looked up and could no longer see them, so I decided to head home, crossing fields, streets, sidewalks and the town's main thoroughfare, which had heavy traffic. I made it back to our apartment building, and rang on the door of the concierge. Though I was alone, I felt a presence with me and was not afraid. My parents, of course, were very upset when they realized what had happened, and had alerted the police.

Like most children, I was very devotional. I had been taught that when I clasped my hands together in prayer, Jesus would come and place his hands around mine. I liked to skip down the road, thinking about Saint Therese of Lisieux, Saint Teresa of Avila and Mother Teresa, who shared the same first name with me and loved Jesus too. I also liked singing "What Child Is This" at the top of my lungs, outside my parents' bedroom, to my father's dismay when he was trying to get some rest!

When I was five years old, I received the sacrament of first holy communion and began to feel the spiritual light. I still remember the holiness of my first midnight mass, and the awe looking at baby Jesus in the crèche. And I still remember the sense of elation, freedom, and joy each sunny Easter morning, when I would wear a fresh new dress and rejoice amidst the blossoming trees and flowers.

I would ask many questions of my catechism teachers.

When I asked them why Jesus was the only one to have two fathers, one in heaven and one on earth, their answer was not fulfilling. I could never get enough of the Bible stories my Mother read to me, and that I continued to read and reread for myself as soon as I was old enough to do so.

My grandmother had taught me the Lord's Prayer and the Hail Mary, which I faithfully repeated, and I cherished a little Bible she gave me that had been hers as a child, along with many cards and pictures of saints, embroidered in paper lace and gold, that had faded with age.

In 1977, we moved to East Fairfield, Vermont, a little village with a covered bridge and a very "small town," insular atmosphere. The contrast with Chantilly was stark. My Mother had longed to find her American roots again, and my Father had agreed to follow her. Like many Europeans, he wanted his chance at the "American dream," and to become an entrepreneur. After investing a lifetime of savings and more, the business my parents had started floundered and we experienced very difficult years. I weathered my way by reading the "Little House on the Prairie" series, by writing poetry and by praying. Laying in bed at night, I tried to acknowledge every saint I knew, but would inevitably fall asleep before getting through my list.

Then when I was about ten, my Mother gave me a book on Greek mythology that I devoured from cover to cover. From that point forward, I could not get the idea of gods and goddesses working with humankind out of my head. I learned all of the stories of the Greek pantheon by heart, which I shared with my sixth grade classmates. I felt especially close to Pallas Athena, Goddess of Truth. She was my favorite. During my childhood years, God's intercession sometimes came as the answer to a prayer. For a long time now, my brother and I had wanted bicycles. My grandparents had offered to buy some but my father adamantly refused. He had seen a reckless driver come around the bend near our home and run a dog over, and his mind was made up. We would never have bicycles!

Dissuading him was impossible so I turned to God and implored him each night for a bicycle. Then, one sunny day the following spring, my brother ran to greet me at the school bus stop, all excited. There was a surprise waiting for us at home: two brand new shining green bikes that my father, of all people, had bought for us on the spur of the moment. I was amazed and my faith was strengthened.

In the early 80s, my Father got his hands on the published works of Nostradamus. He shared with us what he had been reading with great alarm. Of all the dire and most convincing prophecies, the one which concerned me most was that Jerusalem, Paris and Rome were going to be destroyed in 1984.

This grieved me to no end. I could not imagine a world without these beautiful cities. I loved Paris, my birthplace, and I wanted to have the opportunity to visit Rome and Jerusalem, which were surely magnificent as well. I began to pray fervently every night, that these prophecies might not come to pass. I was so relieved when we made it through 1984 with those cities still standing.

The fact that this prophecy of Nostradamus did not come to pass does not make it irrelevant or discredit his work. It is a testament to the power of prayer which should never be underestimated.

In 1993, for example, I read in a journal that four thousand practitioners of Transcendental Meditation from eighty-one countries came to Washington, D.C. to help stop crime, and the rate of violent crime did decrease by twenty-three percent. The odds of this occurring by chance were less than two in one billion.

Over time, I have seen prophecies made and then circumvented by the grace of God, be they from ancient sources, modern-day seers or even from scientific tracking equipment. Time and time again, with the power of prayer, negative prophecies can be mitigated or overturned altogether.

The valley of the shadow of death

When I turned fourteen, I attended high school in Montreal, boarding with host families. These were difficult years. I wanted to fit in and God was not cool. Atheism was the professed creed of the French intellectual elite that I was intended to pattern after. I was struggling with a lack of acceptance and support, which I repressed by indulging in Montreal's nightlife and getting into all kinds of trouble, unbeknownst to my parents. I still managed to receive my French Baccalaureat, a most arduous intellectual rite of passage.

Then, at seventeen, I headed for The American University in Washington, D.C., filled with excitement and trepidation. I would be on my own once again. My parents had to attend to my six younger siblings and could no longer control my strong independent streak. Still, the prospect of starting anew in the alabaster city was daunting for me. I tried hard to squelch the panic I felt when around midnight, the Greyhound bus from Vermont that I was on made an unexpected end of route. I was left scrambling in the New York City terminal, to safeguard the one trunk of belongings that held everything I owned, and to find the next bus.

After settling in Washington, I began to let loose once again. Since Montreal, I had a problem with alcohol, that no one was aware of, and that I would not admit, even to myself. I liked to go dancing with my friends from college. The problem was that after having just a few drinks, I would black out, my body's way of saying "no more."

In these moments on the edge of consciousness, I would simultaneously experience a heightened sense of direction and guidance coming from above me. The vibration was unmistakable. The command was unequivocal and I could not disobey. One of the most dangerous moments was blacking out in the throngs of a Halloween parade in downtown Georgetown, losing the group I was with. Somehow I made it into a cab back to my dorm room.

This presence was guiding me. It was a part of me, yet apart from me. In the fog of numbness when I had lost all sense of compass, its voice resonated through my inner being, and its energy helped me get to safety. Later, when I came to my senses, I was amazed at how I had come through.

On another occasion, I remember heading for a favorite upscale club in the Adams Morgan district. In a flash, I was shown that the world of nightclubs was a world of illusion. I made note of it. This was my higher self, guiding me forward, spurring me on, and I never forgot that superconscious connection. As the psalmist said, "Yea, though I walk through the valley of the shadow of death, I will fear no evil: For thou art with me; Thy rod and thy staff, they comfort me."

The sufis

During my third year of college, I met a woman named Gita who spoke to me of the mystical path of sufism. Something in me stirred again, a deep desire to find God. The sufi path of mysticism made more sense to me than other religious dogma I had come to reject.

After meeting Gita, I started to hang out with Mohammed, an Algerian friend who took upon himself the task of teaching me sufi practices and the words of the prophets. Mohammed and I would go for late drives at night around Washington, where he shared with me all that he knew. Together, we recited the mantra, *La ilaha ilallah*, over and over again, which means, "There is nothing but God."

One night as we were chanting this mantra, faster and faster, I felt an indescribable bliss penetrating my being from head to toe, that was awakening every cell in my body. This bliss was accompanied by an intense heat and an overwhelming joy that lasted for several days. It was hundredfold better than any "high" heretofore experienced. I was converted on the spot. About a week later, while attending a spiritual event in American University's ecumenical chapel, I experienced the bliss again, cleansing me from head to toe.

My husband Brian described the experience of dying to me in similar terms. He was able to recall a past-life death, and said it was like the bursting of a bubble that was containing him here. He likened it to something he had read in the novel *Gates of Fire,* where Steven Pressfield narrates the process of dying as having the breath knocked out of you.

Brian shared that after the initial, uncomfortable shock of the aura bursting and the soul releasing from the body, we experience great bliss if we enter the octaves of light.

In this life, when Brian died as a baby in the early sixties in Saskatchewan, Canada, his aura did not burst. He simply left his body consciously, and was taken up and comforted by a lady with a pink blanket. The love that he experienced was all that he wanted to share when, months later, he learned how to talk.

At the age of twenty-eight, Brian retraced these steps, so to speak, with two out-of-body experiences, one week apart. In the first OBE, the Divine Mother washed his spiritual, etheric body with white light. In the second, angels tuned his etheric body by singing a rising crescendo of musical notes that ended in a sound like high "C."

The etheric body is the spiritual vehicle surrounding the physical form that allows our soul to travel into many levels of the heaven-world, called "etheric plane" by theosophists, so that we can commune with our higher self and download our life's superconscious blueprint. Jesus described the etheric plane when he said, "In my Father's house, there are many mansions."

Through vibration, our soul is polarized and gravitates towards a certain frequency. We can travel to the etheric plane while our body sleeps at night and after we have passed away. We set the sail of our consciousness to go to this plane of higher consciousness through prayers, meditation and good works.

There is also the the astral, or desire plane. This is where our negative emotions and excessive desires play out, the world of relativity that lures us to indulge in "evil," which Mark Prophet said was "energy veil." We can go to the astral plane, either during sleep or at the time of transition.

The astral plane is what the Catholics call purgatory, what the ancient Greeks called Hades and what the Tibetans call bardo in the *Tibetan Book of the Dead*. Like the etheric plane, the astral plane also has many levels. In the higher astral plane reside impostors of the ascended masters that people connect with in a psychic way.

A friend once told me that during an LSD trip, he ended up in the higher levels of the astral plane. It was what people call a "good trip." He could see the heaven-world and the masters on the other side but he was barred from entering in. There are also "bad trips," into the lower astral plane.

The lower levels of the astral plane correspond to the visions of "hell" that Dante and others have described. Our consciousness can get stuck there. That is why it is dangerous to take hallucinogenic drugs that artificially stimulate our spiritual centers, and try to take heaven by force.

No good thing comes from the astral plane. The seeming "best" of the highest levels still falls into a relative good and evil, which directly reflects our inherited subconscious propensities and wrong choices.

After my spiritual awakening, I decided to never drink or get high again. I instinctively knew there could be no compromise, if I were to experience the divine presence. When I went out with my college friends, I would recite 'there is nothing but God" under my breath, while everyone else was partying.

During the days, weeks and months that followed, I learned how to meditate. Then one night, I found myself waking up in the most unusual way. I could hear all of the cells in my body chanting the sufi mantra distinctively, clearly and in unison. I wasn't hearing through my ears. I was hearing through my cells! The singing kept getting louder and louder, and with it I found myself floating upward.

All of a sudden, I became frightened. I had experimented with tapes teaching how to do out-of-body, astral projection when I was in my teens, and had encountered an oppressive feeling of evil. I got out of bed with a jerk. I often wonder what might have happened, had I let this moment fulfill itself completely. I simply didn't have the wherewithal to deal with it then.

Saint Germain and the violet flame

During my senior year in college, I spent a semester in Argentina. Up to that point, I had continued to explore sufism as well as other new-age teachings. I was in search of a guru, a spiritual "personal trainer," and also eager to connect with a group for meditation and spiritual work. A sufi teacher I had met the year before had responded detachedly to my enthusiasm so I was still looking.

Columbus Day weekend 1990, I decided to take a fifteen-hour bus ride to Iguazu falls, one of the wonders of the world bordering Argentina and Brazil. I knew something exciting was about to unfold. I spent the weekend meditating on the rainbows bouncing off the waterfalls, directing the light into my chakras. Then coming home, I met a Brazilian man headed back to Buenos Aires from Rio.

We started to converse about life, driving under starry skies through the pampas. Then, as we were nearing daybreak, I blurted out, "I do meditation," yielding to an urge I had repressed all night to bring up my spiritual quest.

"So do I," he said to my amazement, pulling out a portrait of the ascended master Saint Germain, along with a picture of the Chart of the Presence, that shows a person enfolded in a tube of light under rings of spiritual colors. My friends told me about a group in La Plata, about an hour away from Buenos Aires, that got together to do spiritual work. I decided to drop my other commitments and follow him there. I had no time to waste. Could this be what I was looking for?

We arrived together in La Plata and I met the most welcoming smiling faces. After a hearty vegetarian meal, we gathered in a circle and started to read prayers out loud that invoked the violet flame, a spiritual light that transmutes and consumes negative energy. One of these prayers is,

> "Yo Soy un ser de llama violeta
> Yo Soy la pureza que Dios desea.
> I AM a being of violet fire
> I AM the purity God desires."

We continued to give these prayers for two hours and by the time we were done, I felt light, clear and deeply happy. When we left the meeting, a surge of joyous, buoyant energy accompanied my steps. I had never experienced anything quite like it.

I returned to La Plata week after week and my new friends taught me everything they knew about angels, elohim and ascended masters, as well as about our Mighty I AM Presence, the spirit of God connected to us. We passionately discussed these topics with South American fervor, between sips of yerba mate and honey in a small wooden bowl with a silver straw that we passed around like a peace pipe.

I wanted to learn everything about these teachings that I could get my hands on. I started devouring classic esoteric literature like *The Magic Presence, Unveiled Mysteries* and *The I AM Discourses,* and discovered the magical adventures of people who had interacted with the master Saint Germain, along with the alchemical spiritual formulas he imparted to help transform their lives for the better.

My friends also told me about a woman called Elizabeth Clare Prophet who worked with Saint Germain in the United States. I had never heard of her and was intrigued by their description.

I started invoking Saint Germain's alchemical formulas for self-transformation daily. It was exciting for me to put his teachings to the test, especially after experiencing the violet flame.

Presencia Yo Soy

One spring day, I was walking through La Boca, a colorful, artsy neighborhood of Buenos Aires, taking pictures, when I became aware that a young couple had been following me. All of a sudden, the woman pulled out a handkerchief and insisted on wiping my back because she said there was a mustard stain on my shirt.

I knew that local thieves sprayed tourists with mustard in order to rob them while helping them clean up, so I politely thanked the woman and told her mustard comes off in the wash. Then I walked away, relieved that my purse was intact. I had just exchanged a lot of dollars and had all of my bank and credit cards with me, which was the only way for me to get more funds.

A short time later, while I was waiting for a bus in front of the main train station, I was caught off guard. A young man pointed to the stain on my shirt and the minute I turned around, my wallet was gone. I asked the man to give it back and he denied taking it. Then, I remembered these thieves work in groups. I looked around and saw a man in his forties, dressed in a suit, crossing the street whistling.

My intuition told me this man had my wallet, so I started chasing him. He turned around and when he saw that I was coming after him, started to run too. I ran as fast as I could, dodging all of the collectivo buses and taxis that were coming at us with Latin speed.

"Para le! Stop him!" I yelled, as people watched, but nobody moved. Eventually, I could no longer keep up with him and he started to get lost in the bustle.

This was a real crisis for me, having no money to get home or to finish my stay. I had just learned about the Mighty I AM Presence, the personalized divine presence that hovers above us at all times, surrounded by concentric rings of spiritual energy, I decided to call upon it for help.

"Presencia Yo Soy," I fervently cried, under my breath, as I continued to run. No sooner had the words come out of my mouth that I experienced a renewed burst of energy and spotted the man in the crowd again.

He looked behind and saw me, and decided to give up the chase, though he still had the lead. "Here's your cuero," he said, when I caught up with him, throwing my wallet on the ground.

By that time, a crowd had formed around us. I did not know whether to laugh or cry. My lungs were burning and I was out of breath, but I felt elated because my wallet was intact. I knew that my Mighty I AM Presence had intervened. I was so grateful. I can't even begin to imagine the nightmare it would have been to be stranded in Buenos Aires without money.

Love holds everything together

Travelling through the great deserts of Western Argentina by bus on my way to visit the glacier Perito Moreno, my eyes started to focus on the rocks along the side of the road, and I marveled at how everything was made. In a flash, I understood that love holds everything together. Without love, none of the atoms would stay together and matter would not exist. It was a magical realization. I felt that interconnectedness again in Ushuaia, which is the southernmost tip of the Southern Hemisphere, as well as when we crossed over the beautiful Andean Pass Libertadore on the way to Santiago, Chile.

Jewels in the heart

Back in Buenos Aires, I met the daughter of my host family. She was about my age, sweet and very sophisticated. She was wearing expensive jewelry that was not common for a young adult. I was admiring her jewelry as we were talking, and wondered what it would be like to wear jewels like this.

That night, I found myself waking up to a spiritual experience. I was fully conscious, though my body was sleeping, when God took me inside my heart. There, he showed me three jewels, radiant divine flames of love, wisdom and power, far more beautiful, far more glorious, than any outside gem. Nothing in the world could compare to their awesome, scintillating, intimate and intelligent presence. I had seen the threefold flame of life, God's gift of love so pure. All I could ever want was already mine to cherish as treasures of the heart.

A voice out of heaven

It was early 1991. I didn't want to leave South America. I had fallen in love with that continent. Looking out the window of the plane that was taking me back to the States, tears started rolling down my cheeks. I heard my higher self say, "You will come back. You are going home for training." This gave me comfort and I immediately assumed I would return to South America within six months, after college graduation. Little did I know that my "training" would take at least two decades.

The first sign that greeted me in the JFK airport was an ad from AT&T. "So many things to do, so little time." I couldn't help but groan. I had become accustomed to the South American sense of time and a culture where relationships are more important than stressing to get the job done. I didn't want to reintegrate with the North American lifestyle. Eventually I had to yield to the time constraints and pressures of my senior year in college, with the part-time jobs I juggled to make ends meet.

Back in Washington, I started yearning for a group of spiritually like-minded people that I could connect with. My friends in Argentina had told me of an I AM Temple in New York. I tried to find it, but nothing seemed to gel. I resisted looking into The Summit Lighthouse and the teachings delivered through Mark and Elizabeth Clare Prophet. Even though I wanted to study about ascended masters and meditate and decree with others, I didn't want to join what some people had said was a "cult."

Then, one day, while browsing through a bookstore at Union Station, I came across *The Science of the Spoken Word* by Elizabeth Clare Prophet. I had already perused the Spanish version of the book in a store downtown Buenos Aires. Now, as I flipped to the back, I saw their contact information. I decided to try my chances. I called the number and spoke to someone who connected me to a study group in Washington.

When I contacted the study group, the person on the other end of the phone asked me whether I wanted to be a "Keeper of the Flame" for Saint Germain. My heart stirred and I said yes. I was eager to study more about Saint Germain so I signed up to become a member of the Keeper of the Flame Fraternity. Every month, I received a new lesson in the mail with simple, practical and powerful spiritual tools. Each lesson built upon the last, helping me to work more closely with the invisible brotherhood of masters who overshadow us to steer our human endeavors towards spiritually constructive outcomes.

About the same time, I went to my first spiritual service at the study group and met someone who had visited the organization's headquarters in Montana. I asked this person what her impression was of Elizabeth Clare Prophet. I was curious, having heard so many things. "Look into her eyes and you will see," she said. "When I did, I knew that I had found my teacher."

The following year, I moved to California to pursue a

master's degree in international policy. That winter, I decided to head up to Montana to meet Elizabeth Clare Prophet and look into her eyes for myself. I was wondering what it would be like to be present for a "dictation," where the aura of an ascended master comes over the Messenger to give a teaching.

I soon found out that these dictations, delivered through the power of the Holy Spirit, were a completely different experience from psychic channeling.

A couple of years earlier, a friend of mine had treated me to a "reading" by a renowned Maryland psychic for my birthday. This lady was so "good" that people would line up to wait for her services, sitting in their cars from the wee hours of the morning. During my reading, a lot of trivial information had been brought up. For instance, she told me I was going to soon meet and possibly have a relationship with a blond man.

While our interchange was going on, I had noticed something curious. The more this woman "read" what was going to happen to me, the more I felt a stream of energy siphoning out from me and going straight to her. I wondered what she was taking from me to do her work.

Now during dictations, it was the other way around. My body was filled with light and the spiritual energy was very powerful.

The dictation that stood out the most for me was one by Krishna, the ascended master who is a focus of Hindu bhakti devotion. I was sitting in the back of the room. When the dictation began, the joy and bliss was so intense that I started to laugh and could not stop. The entire congregation was very quiet, sitting in a meditative posture and here I was, laughing until tears rolled out of my eyes. It was the holiest laugh I ever had!

At the end of the conference, I chose to get baptized, and Elizabeth, fondly known as 'Mother,' conducted the ritual. As I stood before her, I looked into her eyes, and it did seem like universes danced within them. Mother beamed a big smile. Then, she placed water and rose petals on my head and started to baptize me, "In the name of the Father, the Mother, the Son and the Holy Spirit."

I noticed a resonance in her voice that was truly extraordinary. The only way to describe it was like a portal into a higher octave. The sound was traveling down a tunnel into the physical plane. It was the voice of God speaking through her. I had never heard anything like this before. It was something you could never forget.

By their fruits shall ye know them

I fell in love with a man that I had met in the cafeteria during that first conference. A few months later, we got married on a beach near Carmel, California. As soon as we had exchanged our vows, a heaviness settled upon me that I was unaccustomed to. Indeed my marriage, based on the euphoria of "love at first sight," proved rocky. I had to stop my university studies and move from California to Chicago so that we could find some work. I was twenty-two years old at the time.

One day, after attending a service at the Chicago Teaching Center, I met someone who said he had been a student of the ascended masters for many years. We started to spend time together. I noticed that when I was with this person, I had a "feel good" buzz. Pretty soon, he started to give me "messages" from the masters. He would say things like, "The elohim are here with you now."

The messages centered around a few themes like how great a person I was and how we could make lucrative business ventures together. They implied that we were more "chosen" by God than others and initially brought comfort to an otherwise challenging time.

Eventually, it became harder and harder for me to hear the subtle inner voice of my higher self. Still, when I did listen, that voice directed me to look at the fruits. Several months had passed now, and none of the business promises had been fulfilled. Eventually, the more time I spent with this person, the less time I engaged in my former spiritual practices.

The rush of energy, or "high," around the messages had waned and I was becoming depleted. I knew that going back to a path of spiritual discipline would be an uphill climb, after the ease of ascended masters seemingly falling into my lap, so it was hard to break away.

One evening, I went back to the teaching center. There was a small closet, no bigger than a broom closet, with a chair, an altar and a large portrait of the ascended master El Morya, who is the representative of God's will. I fervently asked El Morya to be cut free from my association with this person if it was God's will. It wasn't long before I discovered my friend was having an affair with a lady who had also been attracted to his messages and who was helping support him financially. That was the last straw for me.

The following summer, I spoke about the situation to Dr. Marilyn Barrick, a psychologist who was one of Elizabeth Clare Prophet's close assistants. "Why," I asked her, "did I feel so much bliss and light around him initially?"

Dr. Barrick explained that people involved in psychic channeling connect to impostors of the ascended masters and steal the light from your own God Presence because of your free-will involvement with them. You feel your own light mirrored back to you. This light is stolen from you over time, leaving you depleted. I realized that that was also what had been going on during my psychic reading in

Maryland.

False hierarchy stand-ins for the ascended masters coming through most often well-meaning psychic readers lead you down a corridor of dependence upon them. The true teacher leads you to your higher self. As Mother once told me, "My job is to help you reconnect to your Mighty I AM Presence and Holy Christ Self. Once you are connected, my job is done."

Statements my friend used to make, like "The more you serve the light, the more the light will turn around to serve you," are true, but to what end? The light does not turn around to serve ego-enhancing purposes or get-rich-quick schemes that dodge our karma. True, we are all beautiful spiritual beings beloved by God and the masters, but that is not enough. We have fallen from our first state of grace and we must climb back up. Had we no issues to work out, we would already be ascended in the light.

The real master points out the flaws that need correcting so that the soul can be free from the rounds of rebirth. The real master does not numb us with pleasant sophistries that ultimately keep us chained to the astral plane.

I once ran into Elizabeth Clare Prophet in Washington, D.C. I had been going through a hard time and wanted reassurance. I followed her out the door as she was putting on her coat and said, "Mother, I need for you to tell me that the masters love me." She spun around and gave me the fiercest look. Then she said, with a bolt of spiritual fire that penetrated to the core of my being: "Unconditional love is a New Age thing. You have to earn it." I realized that it wasn't actually her, but the master El Morya, who was talking.

I will never forget the encounter. It stunned me. What did this mean, "Unconditional love is a New Age thing?" Wasn't God unconditional love, I pondered?

Years later, through the work that my husband, Brian, and his colleague, psychologist Caroline Hanstke, pioneered, I came to understand that God's love is both conditional and unconditional. People who are looking for unconditional love from the universe without submitting to spiritual accountability are really pursuing pseudo-love. This is the "hippy" love that Mother was referring to when she said "a New Age thing."

God's energy is Father and Mother, Alpha and Omega. You cannot have unconditional love, which is feminine energy, without the masculine counterpart that comes through conditional love. The energy of God as Father exacts a discipline that curbs our lesser self. If we do not move into alignment with God as Father's direction and discipline, we cannot receive God as Mother's unconditional love.

People who reject spiritual discipline for "lovey" self-indulgence end up deluding themselves. They think they have received unconditional love by getting their way when in fact, it was no love at all. The self-spoiling lure of "anything goes" is costing to the soul. The true love of God that flows both conditionally and unconditionally in a yin and yang, figure-eight, complementary pattern sets the soul free.

Many who had been around Elizabeth Clare Prophet could not handle the disciplines or the abruptness of the Father energy coming from El Morya through her. Like children, they started to compare their lot to others, and to look for discrepancies in treatment. Then, when Mother wasn't in her messenger role and indulged in her own human weaknesses, people who had idolized her criticized the double standard.

When we receive a discipline from God, we are freed from errors in our ways that we may have been carrying for lifetimes. No matter how difficult or unpleasant, when we truly embrace the discipline, we feel free from that which the Father energy has separated us from. It is a grace.

A short while after I met Mother, the masters started giving dictations about resolving your psychology. They said that your spiritual progress would ultimately be blocked if you did not look at your issues. I began to see through the idolatry surrounding Mother that, like the rest of us, she had not resolved her psychology. In 1996, in fact, during a series of "darshan" lectures with staff, Mother repeatedly talked about getting to the bottom of our psychology. "This is something we all have to do," she said, including herself.

Mother approached Brian three times and asked him if he would help her work on her psychology. The first time was on a beach in San Diego. The second time was at a hot springs in Bozeman and the third time was during an intermission at the opera. Brian tried to fulfill Mother's request and contact her secretary to set up an appointment, but no response was forthcoming.

"I have to get to the bottom of my psychology," Mother had expressed to him most earnestly.

"You do know you will have to work on your issues with your Father," Brian replied.

"Yes," she said, "I know. I have dealt with him spiritually, mentally and physically, but I have not dealt with him emotionally."

Elizabeth's father was a stern and difficult figure. Mother had taken on, as we all do, negative patterns passed down through childhood training and inherited genes. She now wanted to process these patterns out, especially that which would make her become harsh and authoritarian.

As a messenger, her unresolved psychological patterns had blurred with the intense divine discipline coming from the masters. It was sometimes hard to tell where her father's patterns stopped and where El Morya started.

In my own encounter with Mother, I had been looking for unconditional love from God without having to change for the better. To my surprise, I had received the Father. This divine rebuke, as well as many intense disciplines that followed, struck a blow to my ego.

I tried to not resist the spiritual fire that was coming through to test my metal, even though I could not make out the meaning of the message. In shock, my human conditioning stopped sharply in its tracks. I did not receive the syrupy sympathy and indulgent reassurance that I was looking for. Instead, I received an impetus to come up higher and to stop self-justifying.

I ran into this intense spiritual stripping on another occasion, when I called the "youth hotline" that Mother had established to speak to any young person who needed her guidance. At the time, I confessed to Mother a problem I couldn't seem to get on top of. We didn't talk long and after we hung up, it seemed like bolts of spiritual fire were coursing through my veins all night. Receiving such fire was not without pain, but in the end I got over my issue much faster.

As the years went by and I grew in spiritual understanding, I started to receive expressions of unconditional love from Mother. I was in a completely different state of consciousness and the love of God that I experienced in her presence seemed limitless.

Staying in tune

As I continued to explore esoteric teachings, I discovered that syncopated rhythms found in rock music, rap music and jazz will set you back. Pictures drawn by clairvoyants, as well as experiments on plants, show the detrimental effects of these kinds of rhythm and their accompanying lyrics on our spiritual, mental, emotional and physical nature. If you read the lyrics or contemplate the art that goes hand in hand with many of these songs, it becomes obvious that they do not tether your consciousness to the etheric plane, but rather to the darker levels of the astral plane. Still, I was attached to my favorite bands and did not want to make that shift.

I spoke to a Summit Lighthouse minister about this, who suggested I stop listening to music for an entire month, and then reconsider. I took her advice. A month after my music fast, when I began to play my favorite bands again, I noticed that energy was leaking out of my base-of-the-spine chakra. I also noticed that some of the more intense music hurt my heart chakra.

From that day forward, I started to listen to other forms of music like classical, folk and Eastern. These lift you up without having a jagged effect on the chakras.

The gas chamber

In 1993, I joined the army with my first husband, and left for basic training at Fort Jackson in the sweltering heat of a South Carolina summer. I was twenty-three years old. When it became apparent that our recruiter had enlisted us with misleading information, the army basically made a deal with us. If I stayed on, my husband could go home.

I was willing to continue and to tough it out. I knew that if I served four years, the army would pay off my student loans. It was an offer I could not refuse.

Even though I had a strong sense of patriotism, I was not cut out for the the loss of personal freedom nor for the levels of mental, emotional and physical abuse that we were put through. Knowing the power of the spoken word, I couldn't bear chanting, "Boots inside the head, kick them till they're dead," or "Mama, mama, don't you cry, your little girl is gonna die" over and over again, while we marched through swampy woodlands.

It wasn't until I was in the army that I realized how much I despised war, along with guns, grenades and bayonettes. I had naively thought that by signing up for an office job, I would avoid combat training.

One day, as we started to assemble and disassemble M-16s, I had a flashback to another time. I was sorting out thick jungle brush with an M-16 in my hands, and I remembered that at the end of that M-16 was death. This led me to having a panic attack.

I had to get out now, but how? Leaving without a discharge meant going AWOL, a crime punishable in military court. The last thing I wanted to do was spend a few years in military jail.

I started to pray without ceasing. Then on a Sunday morning, when we marched into church, I was prompted to go to confession. I burst into tears in front of the chaplain.

"You're not here for confession," the chaplain said.

"No, "I admitted. "I can't stay here. I can't stand even the thought of killing."

The chaplain told me he would help me and went to see my commanding officers. I prayed my way through several more nightmare weeks. In the meanwhile, a dreaded event loomed on the horizon.

Our platoon was going to the gas chamber. I had heard about it from others. You put on a gas mask and enter a chamber filled with tear gas. Once inside, you have to remove the gas mask for as long as the drill sergeant, who still has one on, determines. The gas burns your eyes, lungs and skin and when soldiers are finally allowed to exit the building, they are throwing up with tears and mucus running down their faces.

I knew our drill sergeants would not be letting us out easily. I had seen soldiers pushed beyond their limits in other exercises, to the place of passing out or breaking bones.

Now even though the sergeants knew that I was pending discharge, they would not exempt me. I had to surrender: "Father, if this cup cannot pass away from me unless I drink it, your will be done."

We drove to the training site and were sitting on a bench, waiting for our turn, when God answered. Our sergeant told us that because of a mix-up, there was not enough tear gas for our group. This was something that had never happened before. My sense of relief was out of this world.

That same night, after thirty-three days, my discharge papers came through. Lying in my bed I closed my eyes and cried, in gratitude and to relieve the tension. All of a sudden, I saw, with my inner eye, a purple mist. Behind this mist lay a placid pond of deep emerald on which grew a large and beautiful lotus. The outer petals were soft pink, the center petals golden. Upon the lotus sat a Buddha. In contemplation, he raised his arms and embraced all of the stars of cosmos as their light pierced the night. His peace was complete. He was God, the beginning and the ending, the creator and sustainer of all worlds. I then saw that the lotus on the pond where Buddha sat was in my heart and that there was no separation, no fear, only harmony, peace and a deep abiding faith.

Three days later, I left the base. My first impulse was to run down the street as fast as I could. Being free again was exhilarating. Never had I appreciated it so much.

The burning coal

In 1994, I spent a couple of months in Washington, D.C. to further my training in journalism. One Sunday morning, I was listening to the recording of a dictation by Justinius, Captain of Seraphic Bands, that Elizabeth Clare Prophet had delivered many years before. The seraphim are large, six-winged angels that were seen by the prophet Ezekiel. They form a choir in the heaven-world and are great healers.

In the dictation, Justinius spoke of the seraphim who will place a burning coal on your tongue. This spiritual initiation is recorded in the Book of Exodus. In my heart, I told Justinius that I wanted to receive the burning coal. Even though we were only listening to a recording, when the dictation came to a close, I felt my tongue and mouth tingling with an intense sensation, just like when you burn your tongue on a hot drink! It was amazing to feel it so physically.

Driving on empty

I learned how to drive in my early twenties and did not have much experience with cars. It was 1995 and I was now living in Minneapolis. On the weekends, I set out to give spiritual lectures in local librairies, which were well attended.

This was a clear blue Sunday afternoon, and the lecture was scheduled about forty miles away in a library on the other side of town. I was driving there with a friend.

I headed down the highway without noticing that we were out of gas. Not long after, the car stopped as it does when empty. This was a busy highway so I pulled over to the left, near a concrete divider, sure that it was a mechanical problem caused by spiritual "opposition" to the lecture. I started making intense calls to God and the ascended masters to help me get there no matter what.

After the calls, the car started up, and we continued to drive for a few more miles, until it puttered out again. I pulled over and made more calls. The car started up and again went a few more miles. Then it stopped so I made more calls, that nothing would deter us from getting to the lecture hall. The car stopped and started again at least six or seven more times, until we reached a gas station a block from our destination. That was when I finally realized that it needed gas!

Incredibly, we made it to the lecture on time, and more

incredible still, the fact that we drove about forty miles on a completely empty tank. Looking back, I smile at the fact that I thought my mechanical problem was spiritual opposition when it was only a matter of putting gas in the tank. Thank goodness God supplied the difference.

Archangel Michael, help me!

Over the holidays, my younger sister Marie came up from New Orleans to visit. We decided to head to Montana so she could attend a New Year's conference and experience an ascended master dictation. Before getting in the car, I told Marie about calling to Archangel Michael for protection, and taught her the fiat, "Archangel Michael, help me, help me, help me!"

Within a short time, we had an opportunity to put the fiat to the test. We were driving at highway speed when the car hit a patch of ice and started to spin. There were cars coming both ways and we had lost complete control of the vehicle. At that point, we shouted, "Archangel Michael, help me, help me, help me!" The car made a 360-degree turn, then stabilized in the right lane, heading in the right direction, without hitting any other cars.

Marie and I laughed with joy and relief. She told me that up to that point, she hadn't been sure about Archangel Michael or any of the other teachings I had shared with her, like whether it was helpful to decree.

An angel in a pickup truck

On our way home from the conference, we decided to drive through the night to get back to Minneapolis for Marie's flight. We took turns driving and at about midnight, I fell asleep.

It was extremely cold and pitch dark on the highway. We were in eastern Montana, which is very barren country, and the roads were covered with a thick sheet of ice. All of a sudden, Marie accidentally jerked the steering wheel.

I woke up, startled, as we headed down a fifteen-foot ditch. The car softly stopped at the bottom, lodged inside a snowbank. We were stuck. We hadn't seen any traffic for a long, long time and the car did not have much gas left.

I stepped outside the car and realized we were in a life-and-death situation, so I started to call to God and to Archangel Michael for immediate help. We had no time to lose.

Within a minute or so of making the call, a man showed up in a pickup truck. He was wearing a flannel plaid shirt, overalls and some kind of cap on his head. He was very friendly and completely calm.

"You girls are lucky I stopped by," he said, "because even highway patrol isn't out tonight in these road conditions." He pulled out a tow rope and told me to go inside his truck to warm up. I sat down and waited, listening to the country music that was gently playing. Then he told Marie, "Go check up on your sister because she is very worried." Neither of us had told him we were sisters.

The man pulled the car out of the ditch and told us he would follow us to Miles City, where we must stop and get a hotel room. We thanked him, got in the car and drove off. I could see him in the rearview mirror, following us. We were the only two cars on the road. Then, as we reached the first signs for Miles City, I looked up in the mirror and he was gone.

Since that trip, I have driven through Miles City many times. There is no road that exits the highway where this took place.

The yellow ray

It was summertime and I was attending another conference, this time in the Heart of the Inner Retreat, an alpine meadow above the Summit Lighthouse headquarters. Dozens of large white tents had been raised and thousands of spiritual seekers from around the world were gathering to hear new mystical messages and teachings. On this particular day, the masters of the yellow ray of divine wisdom and illumination were giving dictations. First the Elohim Apollo and Lumina, followed by Archangel Jophiel and Christine, and then by the master Lanto.

In the months preceding the conference, I discovered that I suffered from a form of dyslexia that had probably been there since childhood, but was most certainly exacerbated by my partying years. This dyslexia manifested in a number of ways and also affected my short-term memory. It was hard for me to remember a set of instructions. My brain would fog over. This had become a real handicap for me in my work with small children at a daycare center.

I visited specialized therapists and diligently did "brain gym" exercises, but could not get my eyes to turn full circle, which indicates a disconnection between the right and left sides of the brain, among other things. I wanted my brain to be restored to wholeness.

Before the dictations began, I asked the yellow-ray masters to heal my brain. After the dictations, I was so involved in the moment that I completely forgot about my prayer. I heard my higher self saying, "Aren't you going to check?"

"Check what?" I thought, and then remembered. I lifted my eyes and tried to make them turn, first in a clockwise, then in a counterclockwise direction, like I had many times before. This time, they were no longer stuck.

I tried again and again and sure enough, my eyes could make a complete, uninterrupted circle, which I understood from the therapy meant the brain connections had been restored. I was so grateful for God's forgiveness and willingness to make us whole, in spite of our shortcomings. It felt like a new lease on life.

Blessing food

Blessing food and the "laying on" of hands are ancient spiritual traditions. Food, like our bodies, is mostly made up of water. Water molecules, as Dr. Masaru Emoto has demonstrated, crystallize according to vibrational patterns and energies. The hands have secret-ray chakras in the middle of the palms. Through these chakras, spiritual energy flows to bless and to heal.

I started to place my hands over my food before eating. Sometimes I would say a prayer and, at other times, I would simply send a conscious intent over the plate, thinking "Charge this food with light!"

The more I got into the habit of blessing my food, the more I noticed the energy coming through the center of my palms. I also noticed less light coming through when I blessed healthy, whole foods and more light descending over fast food, microwaved food and food prepared around negative energy. The light coming through my hands became an indicator of the quality of food I was about to partake in.

How comforting it is to know that when you can't eat in an optimal way, God will make up for it with light when you bless your food.

Double rainbows

During the summer of 1995, my first marriage had reached a point of no return. Even though my husband and I diligently tried to work on our relationship, the more issues we resolved, the less karma we had binding us together. Eventually, there was no energy left to keep us from going our separate ways. We parted amicably and, to save money, I spent days in a legal library in downtown Minneapolis drafting our divorce documents so we wouldn't have to hire a lawyer.

The process was very painful for me, letting go of future plans, dreams, expectations and a sense of familiarity I had come to depend on. My birthday was approaching, July 21, and I was most burdened, so I asked Mother Mary to give me a sign of God's love for my birthday, something I would know was from her.

Several days passed. Then on my birthday, some friends and I gathered at the outside terrace of a local restaurant to celebrate. In the middle of our meal, a tornado warning was issued and we were all encouraged to go into a nearby shelter.

The sun was still warm and bright, so a few of us decided to stay outside and watch the incredible cloud display amassing in the sky. All of a sudden, the most magnificent double rainbow we had ever seen appeared in the sky. Both rainbows were perfectly formed and every color was absolutely brilliant, in an almost surreal way.

We were gazing at the sky in awe, when one of my friends tugged me on the sleeve and said, "Therese, I have to tell you. This is from Mother Mary for your birthday." It was so touching. I had not told anyone about my prayer and had even forgotten about it myself.

Shiva! Shiva! Shiva!

I had often wondered what dreams were all about. My husband Brian helped me to understand, based on spiritual teachings he has read that have been confirmed by his own experiences.

Our souls can either go to the etheric plane in our etheric double, or to the astral plane in our astral double. The etheric double and the astral double are envelopes of energy inside the aura that our soul travels with as it leaves the physical body.

Brian explained that the etheric plane is actually a part of our physical plane, but it vibrates at a higher frequency than what our eyes can see. The etheric plane corresponds to the level of the heart chakra in our body. Now our soul resides in the seat-of-the-soul chakra, which is located right below the belly button. Between the two is the solar plexus chakra, that ties into our emotions, or astral nature.

To go to the etheric plane, the soul must rise through the energy vortex of the solar plexus chakra. Like a drop of oil rising to the surface of water, our souls must rise through the astral element to get to the heart chakra and access the etheric plane. Oftentimes, we get stuck in the astral plane on the way to or from the etheric retreats and we tend to remember the astral experiences. It is harder to remember the etheric experiences because they are more subtle.

That is why it is important to pray before falling asleep,

like we were taught as children. We can call to Archangel Michael, Jesus and other ascended masters for protection. I still remember the prayer that I recited as a child,

> "Now I lay me down to sleep
> I pray the Lord my soul to keep
> If I should die before I wake
> I pray the Lord my soul to take."

Whether asleep or at the time of transition, we do need this protection.

In the etheric plane, we visit ascended master and angelic retreats where we receive instruction. Most of them are congruent with our atmosphere at about 30,000 feet, the altitude that airplanes fly. One is congruent with the Grand Teton Mountain and one is beneath the waters of the Pacific ocean. There are also etheric cities around the globe that Gustav Dore saw and painted, where elemental spirits form great cathedrals and other beautiful structures almost effortlessly.

When I was pregnant with my third child, I started to create illustrations of ascended master retreats. I could feel my unborn child's support from the etheric plane, where souls abide before birth. He was helping me to tweak each image until the vibrational frequency most closely captured the essence of that plane.

In the etheric retreats, masters and angels commune with unascended mankind in a climate of mutual goodwill and respect. They outpicture the consciousness of the New

Jerusalem that was described in the Book of Revelation: "And God shall wipe away all tears from their eyes; and there shall be no more death, neither sorrow, nor crying, neither shall there be any more pain: for the former things are passed away."

We spend about a third of our life sleeping and have an opportunity to journey into the etheric octaves during that time, even if we don't remember upon awakening. We also can go there for training between embodiments. Brian has explained that in the retreats, the masters do not simply give general instructions in large classes. They also work with us on an individual basis to help us download the superconscious blueprint from our God-presence, the next best "right step" for our lifestream. That is why it is so key for us to get there. It is personally relevant to our day-to-day life.

Our consciousness before bedtime determines where we go. It is harder to end up in the etheric octaves if we just had a fight or watched a violent movie. That's why Jesus admonished to his disciples, "Let not the sun go down upon your wrath." Sleeping in a messy, dirty room, and not taking a shower can also have an impact, as does drinking liquor, smoking or eating heavy foods.

All of these habits attract astral entities to us, making it easier for us to gravitate to their level when we fall asleep. Many forms of evil do try and attack us on the astral plane, including our own human negative momentums, because we are more vulnerable when we are out of the body.

One night in my sleep, I became aware of the presence of a UFO trying to abduct me on the astral plane. It was a terrifying experience and I felt overpowered by the evil coming from that ship. I knew that my soul was in danger and I turned to God for help.

Still sleeping, I remembered to call to Shiva, the destroyer of evil in the Hindu Trinity. Even though I felt weakened by my sleep state, I started to shout "Shiva! Shiva! Shiva!" With this fiat, I became impermeable to their energy. The danger passed and I woke up, back in my body.

Some people in the new age movement see UFOs as benevolent. Others believe that ascended masters travel on their ships. This was the case for many of my South American friends.

UFOs use a technology far more advanced than what we have. They are able to change frequency and weave in and out of the astral plane. When I was in Argentina, I visited the Ubitorco, a mountain area that seemed to be frequented by a lot of UFOs, and I was able to watch them at a distance. One minute they were there, the next minute they were not and then they reappeared again. That night, my friends had decided that as an adventure, we would sleep in a rock formation at the top of the mountain to see if one of those ships would take us on board too. Aside from waking up in the freezing cold, and having one of the most uncomfortable nights of my life, nothing else happened and no master came to get us.

Looking back, this was not only silly but spiritually unwise. Most UFOs, or "naves" as they are called in the southern hemisphere, are not benevolent. People who have suffered from abductions and UFO experimentation know this firsthand. And those who purport that UFOs carry ascended masters have a psychic vibration associated with the astral plane. They are false hierarchy impostors of the Great White Brotherhood who will seek to drain your energy instead of exalting your soul.

The ascended masters do not need spaceships to work with us. The presence of God speaks to us through the "still, small voice" in the heart which is the true path of light embraced by saints and adepts of all ages. Neither would ascended masters come to "save" us on spaceships. The salvation that the Brotherhood of Light directs us towards is the salvation of the soul through service to life, not taking off in a spaceship.

Those who have used spaceships to save themselves in ages past, like during the sinking of Atlantis, were nephilim "gods" like Anu, Enki and Enlil. These fallen ones made themselves "supreme lords of the sky," as recorded in the Sumerian texts and in the Book of Enoch.

They are not of the light. They are impostors of the light. Any who follow in their wake using UFO and psychic phenomena lead you down a path of spiritual enslavement. I remember the pictures my South American friends were passing around of UFOs creating figures of Alpha and Omega in the night sky. Everyone thought it was the most fascinating spiritual demonstration.

The true teacher leads you to permanent reunion with God under your own vine and fig tree, the contact with your higher self that is your rightful inheritance.

In a time when so many voices are clamoring for attention, professing to represent the ascended masters through all manner of channeling and UFO thralldom, it is important to remember this precept: The path of the ascended masters and the Great White Brotherhood is the path followed by saints, East and West. The vibration is pure, clear, and sharp like truth itself. It separates itself out from the sickly sweet, sticky dross of psychic phenomena.

Focuses of light

A talisman is an object that is imbued with spiritual energy and creates a hookup to the etheric plane. Since the beginning of time, people have used talismans to protect, heal and ward off evil spirits. Some talismans are small, like a charged crystal, a piece of jewelry or rosary beads.

There are also historical objects like the shroud of Turin, Juan Diego's tilma, the relics of saints and the sword that pierced Jesus, which Hitler, adept at black magic, was hell-bent on acquiring. Talismanic power motivated the Knights of the Round Table in their metaphysical quest to find the Holy Grail. And spring water blessed by Mother Mary in Lourdes has healed people for more than one hundred years.

Talismanic energies also bless larger edifices, from the ancient pyramids and obelisks of Egypt, to the mysterious spiral staircase in New Mexico's Loretto chapel.

In my travels, I specifically experienced talismanic energy over the Statue of Liberty and the Washington Monument. While living in D.C., I loved to take the elevator to the top of the Washington Monument, even if it meant waiting an hour in line beforehand.

While tourists shuffled in and out of the small observatory, admiring the view, I would bask in the strong currents of spiritual energy that emanated from the top. These currents of divine energy reminded me of the fire under a hot-air balloon. Standing in them, it seemed like you just might lift off!

Years later, when I visited the Statue of Liberty, I felt a similar sensation as we stepped out onto Ellis Island. The spiritual radiation under my feet was so strong that it seemed like the ground was not solid.

These monuments and others hold an important spiritual balance for the nation and for the earth. They provide a chalice for a more than ordinary measure of God's light to be anchored in key places on the physical plane.

A special clearance

After my divorce, I moved to Montana and started working for a public relations firm in Bozeman. One of our clients included a non-profit group called Citizens for a Strong America. It was summer, 1996, and I had an important project to finish, a booklet promoting America's need for missile defense. The task was arduous, compiling information from hundreds of articles, often working long hours overtime.

Saint Germain and other ascended masters had spoken of the need for a strong defense in their dictations and I was glad to be of service. Still, I would have preferred to attend Summit University, a retreat sponsored by The Summit Lighthouse that my sister Marie was attending.

Every weekend, I would drive down to visit Marie and other friends who were at the retreat. Then every Monday, I would drive back to work, wishing I didn't have to.

By the end of the summer, the booklet was completed and it was also time for the Summit University clearance. The clearance was a special event, where students could be spiritually cleared of a number of obstacles and astral entities.

I really wanted to attend this event but I knew it was out of the question since I wasn't enrolled in the program. To compensate, I asked Marie if she would be willing to take a picture of me in her purse so that I could be included energetically. Then, I wrote a letter to every divine being I could think of. I asked them to consider clearing me through the picture, since I couldn't officially attend the event, and since I had worked so hard on the missile defense booklet. I burned the letter, which is a way to send it to the etheric octave.

A couple of days later, Elizabeth Clare Prophet made an announcement to the local community. For the first time in the history of Summit University, the clearance was going to be open to people in the area. Each one's clearance, she said, would be according to their personal service in recent months.

I participated in the clearance in person, standing in one of the first rows, and I definitely felt charged with light and a renewed sense of purpose. I was so grateful to the masters and angels who had answered the letter I had written, in an even better way than hoped for.

The river

On a hot day later that summer, I set out with some friends to go tubing down the Yellowstone River. I had never done this before, but my friends were regulars at it. We were each sitting on inner tubes, and no one had a life jacket. We started downstream, having the time of our life, bobbing up and down in the splashing rapids.

After we passed the first set of rapids, the current separated me from the group and I started to lag behind. All of a sudden, there was a huge boulder just below the surface. Before I could steer away, the water swept me into a giant hole. My inner tube flew into the air and I was engulfed in a powerful whirlpool that was way over my head. Being a good swimmer, I started to tread water but the whirlpool was too strong. I struggled to come up for air but no matter how hard I tried, I could not reach the surface.

Soon all of my energy was spent. I had no strength left and was sucked down into the hole. Everything was dark around me and I felt completely defeated. I knew I had to give up my life even though it didn't seem like the right timing.

"The fallen ones have finally got me," I thought, referring to the force of darkness, and I became acutely aware that a significant part of me would be staying in the bottom of the river. It was my not-self, impermanent and unreal, that I had identified with. This jarring realization was even more disturbing than the physical experience of drowning and I finally did let go.

At that point, time and space collapsed and I found myself on top of the river, a couple of yards away from the whirlpool. I was stunned. I did not experience my body moving from the bottom to the top of the river and had no idea how I got there. I started to swim frantically so I would not get sucked into the whirlpool again, having no tube to hang onto.

One of my friends, Geron, who happened to be a lifeguard, was floating by. He had been leading up the rear when the accident happened. He knew that if he jumped in, we would both drown so he watched me struggle and go under. Then, when I surfaced, he said it was like an angel had picked me up.

Away from the whirlpool, Geron reached out to me with his inner tube and helped me stay calm. As the two of us swam to shore through more rapids, I felt a peaceful light shine upon me. Even though I was still in shock, I knew I would be safe.

Later, I went to the emergency room to get checked out. I was all right physically, but it took me several months to process what had happened mentally, emotionally and spiritually.

A perfect fit

Elizabeth Clare Prophet was selling some of her clothing and personal belongings as a church fundraiser. I was all excited, since I love to shop, but my budget didn't give me much leeway. Most of the dresses and altar clothes were beyond my means, but I really didn't want to leave the sale empty-handed.

Peering through the clothing racks, my eyes fell upon a dress that must have been at least 35 years old. It was an early 1960s style, made of white cotton weave with a long train that went three feet beyond my height. The dress was badly stained and yellowed. It had an undergarment of bright pink satin that could not fit me, but would fit my sister Marie.

Since it was within my budget, I bought it and headed home to see how it would wash. It would take a lot of bleach to take the stains out, which made me a little nervous, but my intuition kept nudging. I poured the bleach in, said some prayers and voila! It came out of the wash cycle white as snow.

I was even more nervous about putting the dress in the dryer. Still, my intuition kept nudging. I really didn't want the dress to shrink, since it was already a tight fit, so I said some prayers while it tumbled. Lo and behold, it came out fitting perfectly. More amazing yet, the long train, and nothing else, had shrunk about three feet to fit my height exactly. Now, the dress was a perfect fit.

Elizabeth had worn this dress in a picture with Mark Prophet that was published on an album about twin flames in love. Around the same time as I found this dress, Brian, my husband-to-be, whom I hadn't yet met, was given that picture by a friend to help him attract the person he would marry. A few years later when we finally got together, he was astonished to know that that dress had been hanging in my closet all the while!

The body of Christ

One night while I was sleeping, I was shown a spiritual umbilical cord that tied me to Christ as a higher spiritual awareness. This Christ essence was a vortex of energy. Then I noticed that from this vortex of energy, umbilical cords of light also reached down to many other people, and reached up to those who had ascended.

I understood that I was looking at the body of Christ, the divine consciousness that ties us together and makes us one, as above so below. I also understood that through these pathways of light, the body of Christ is broken for the many. Now I could appreciate the inner meaning behind the words, "brothers and sisters in Christ."

A few years earlier, while working on a master's degree in international policy, I was selected for a State Department internship at the American Embassy in Lagos, Nigeria. The timing did not work out and I ended up in London for the summer. Still, I had to endure a high-level security clearance, where everything in my life was scrutinized.

The State Department sent an inspector to the little apartment I shared with a roommate. He went through all of my belongings. I was especially nervous when he examined the portable altar that was standing on my bookshelf, with pictures of the ascended masters Jesus, Kuthumi, El Morya and Saint Germain.

Instead of being puzzled or judgmental, he simply remarked, "It's amazing how many different ways you can portray Christ."

I nodded in agreement. I was relieved, and never forgot his words. Christ has many faces. Each of us is one of them.

The Eastern teachings have a name for the connections of light that form the body of Christ. They call it the antahkarana, the web of light that links all sentient beings together.

One night, I was camping with my family in Jackson Hole, Wyoming, right outside the Grand Teton National Park. It was a beautiful starry night and I went for a walk. In my head, I started to complain to God about someone I had issues with. As I looked at the brilliant night sky and the endless starry bodies, I felt my higher self whispering to me, "You may disagree with this person's human self but her soul holds an important position in the antahkarana of light. Would you deny her that?"

The answer of course, was no, and in time, I began to see that even when we find fault with someone's personality, God in us champions their soul. Even when we dislike each other at a human level, we are still connected and made worthy through Christ.

Holy Christ Self above me

From the universal body of Christ, a Christ self individuates for each one of us. This Christ self is our higher self, who evolves in heaven while our soul evolves on earth.

Following a dictation in the Heart of the Inner Retreat, I looked up and saw my Christ self. He appeared to me as a young man with shoulder-length, blond hair, like an Arthurian knight, and he was dressed in ruby and pink garments.

Our Christ self is the spiritual bridegroom Jesus spoke of. Whether we wear a man or a woman's body in life, our Christ self forms the masculine, positive polarity balance for our soul's feminine, negative polarity. He holds a balance for us in heaven while we journey here on earth.

Our soul is destined to fuse with our Christ self through a divine alchemy described in the Book of Revelation as the marriage of the Lamb. This is an initiation which can precede the ascension.

"Let us be glad and rejoice and give Him glory, for the marriage of the Lamb has come, and His wife has made herself ready. And to her it was granted to be arrayed in fine linen, clean and bright, for the fine linen is the righteous acts of the saints. Then he said to me, "Write: 'Blessed are those who are called to the Marriage Supper of the Lamb!' "

Jesus spoke about preparing for this initiation during his Galilean mission. He taught a parable about ten virgins who need to have their lamps trimmed and filled with oil when the bridegroom comes. He taught another parable about a marriage feast where a guest is cast out because he is not wearing a wedding garment. Both of these parables highlight the importance of spiritual preparation. The lamps held by the virgins are a metaphor for the chakras of the body, that need to be filled with light. The wedding garment is a seamless mantle of light in the aura woven through good works and devotion to God, that enfolds the soul, magnetizing her through the heart of Christ back to the I AM Presence.

Angel of the Presence

On a clear and beautiful morning as I was walking down the cobbled streets of Georgetown, I gave a prayer called the "Tube of Light" that invokes the blessings and protection of the Mighty I AM Presence. I could clearly feel a shower of light descending upon me from above, and the sensation of walking inside a cylinder of light-substance.

Surrounding the Mighty I AM Presence is a "causal body" made of concentric rings of rainbow light. In the center resides a divine intelligence, which is actually a spiritual being. The ascended masters call it the Angel of the Presence.

When Jesus taught that "one star differeth from another in glory," he was explaining that no two people have identical causal bodies. Each rainbow ray is actually a frequency of divine energy. The blue color, for example, holds the frequency of good will. The green holds the frequency of abundance and healing. and the pink holds the frequency of love. In each subsequent lifetime, the good works that we do are anchored in our causal body as a measure of light. They are the treasures stored up in heaven that Jesus spoke of.

A soul who, lifetime after lifetime, engages in healing work, for example, will have a larger band of green in their causal body than somebody else. Souls who have demonstrated love over and over again in their interactions with others will have a larger pink band. And older souls who have evolved through more lifetimes than others also have larger causal bodies. They have had more time to qualify and anchor the divine energy allotted to them.

One night after exercising the science of the spoken word and doing many decrees, I closed my eyes. All of a sudden, I was able to see my Angel of the Presence. For me, it manifested as a most holy feminine presence dressed in white raiment. Filigree threads of light emanated from her being. I knew that she was me, and yet she was not the "me" that I am familiar with, the ego self that I identify with and have often defended.

Seeing this presence made me realize that so much of who we are is not who we think we are, and that we exist and evolve on multiple levels of consciousness, hidden from our outer awareness and human personality.

Violet flame blazing

I was trying to get in contact with Elizabeth Clare Prophet by mail and was told to send a photograph so she could evaluate the state of my aura. I decided to give extra violet flame decrees to dissolve as much undesirable substance from my aura as possible. Then I went in to get my picture taken with a Polaroid camera, hoping for the best.

My mouth dropped when I looked at the background. It was filled with violet flames, even though I was standing against a bare white wall!

On another occasion, Brian and I were driving down Malibu, California, when I asked him if he would take a picture. He turned into the nearest parking lot and took a picture of me against the ocean. When the photograph was developed, I was standing in a brilliant ring of light, formed by the sun, like the solar ring we call for in our prayers.

Photographic film can capture spiritual manifestations that cannot be seen with the naked eye. When my first daughter was born, I took a picture of her while sitting down. The photograph came out with very defined white spirals that could not have been created by anything but spiritual light. This happened more than once.

Now in the age of digital cameras, I do not know whether such photographs can still be made, so I treasure the ones that I have as a tangible focus of the world of spirit, merging with our own.

Minuteman for Saint Germain

Minuteman: An armed man pledged to be ready to fight on a minute's notice just before and during the Revolutionary War in the United States. The recruiting standards for minutemen included personal courage, loyalty, duty, respect, selfless service, honor and integrity.

Herbert Beigel was an unforgettable character. I met him at the Chicago Teaching Center in the winter of 1992. He was a tall, handsome, elderly gentleman already in his eighties, with a twinkle of mischief in his bright blue eyes, and a smile you couldn't help but smile with. Herbert was quite a character. He always dressed in pastel suits, crowned with a royal blue, felt top hat. He wore great big gold rings on his fingers, encrusted with jewels and ascended master insignias like the Maltese cross.

Herbert was determined to reverse the aging process through the power of prayer. For the fifteen or so years that I knew him, he did indeed seem younger every time I saw him.

Herbert had studied the ascended master teachings for six or seven decades, day in and day out. He had served as the right hand man of Lotus, the messenger of the I AM Movement, for many years, before meeting Elizabeth Clare Prophet. He often told stories of how he and other fellow students decreed several hours each night for more than four years straight during World War II, enlisting the heavenly hosts to shorten the course of the war and to secure a victory for the Allies.

Herbert never missed a service and always sat in the same chair, to arc the light from the altar. He had experienced live dictations for decades and seemed to remember every spiritual dispensation that had ever been given by an ascended master. He also knew his Bible cover to cover and would quote how the scriptures fit with ascended master teachings.

Herbert refused to see anything but perfection made manifest, almost obstinately. His favorite expression was, "It has no power!" and he would say this in the face of any adversity or setback. That was his greatest strength. He never wavered from his principles or from the letter of the law and would not tolerate any infraction of ascended master principles.

Despite his seeming eccentricities, Herbert had great generosity. He let me stay with him several times and completely funded a conference when I had no money to go. He was an astute businessman who had made his money renovating rundown properties in Chicago. He told me that on at least three occasions, he had lost his entire fortune and had to build it back up from scratch.

Herbert would invite me to sit on the atomic accelerator, a chair he built replicating the atomic accelerator described in Saint Germain's retreat, where people revitalize during soul travel at night. Sitting in Herbert's altar room on this golden chair in the form of a flame, surrounded by myriad focuses and larger-than-life portraits of the masters, you could really feel the presence of God flowing through.

Herbert also taught me to see the photons of light that dance in the atmosphere. He told me this was the substance from which masters and adepts would precipitate whatever they needed.

Herbert often spoke of how important it was to sustain your decree momentum. He would explain to me that when people stopped giving decrees, the energy they were dealing with did not let up accordingly and would swallow them up. He said he had seen this time and time again when someone left the teachings and turned bitter against the ascended masters. The saddest example was that of his first wife, whom he had loved dearly.

Herbert confided that in her service to God, she had reached the status of an archangel. She would decree two hours a day just to get warmed up. She and Elizabeth were close friends, and their children, who were of similar age, liked to play together.

One day, his wife became jealous of Elizabeth and couldn't understand why she could not be the Messenger. This started her on a downward spiral. She stopped doing her decrees and, eventually, stopped following ascended master teachings. She divorced Herbert when he would not follow suit and finished her life with all of his money, cruising the Mediterranean. Still, she was not happy and when she passed on, Herbert seemed to indicate that she was trapped in the astral plane.

The last time I saw Herbert, he took my hand in his. As we sat together, I felt a great current of electric light sweeping through me. He made his transition a few months later, and I have no doubt he has become an ascended master, minuteman for Saint Germain, one with his many friends of Light.

A *"near death" experience*

During the winter of 1996, I received a phone call from my family in France telling me that my beloved grandfather was ill. He had been ill before but this time, I knew I had to hop on a plane. I took a leave from work and left Montana the next day.

After we landed, I went straight to the hospital room where he was laying. He was barely breathing. The skin on his face had turned waxy and grey and his eyes were lifeless. My grandmother was crying and a cousin, who was a medical doctor, said nothing more could be done.

I went over and touched my grandfather's hand. All of a sudden, his eyes jumped back into their sockets and he recognized me. It was a very moving moment, which astonished everyone in the room. Still, he could not move or talk, except to ask for water, which he was not even able to drink.

I went home that evening, certain that he would pass away during the night. I stayed up all night, making intense prayers for him that invoked the angels of the ruby ray of God's love. I also told God that I wanted to offer myself to give birth to him, when it would be his time to come back.

I had brought with me a stainless steel sword with the words "Archangel Michael" engraved on it, used to remove entities and to clear negative energy. There is something about the metal stainless steel that penetrates through the astral plane and can cut through astral entities that seek to drain us of our light. When we carefully wield a stainless steel sword or knife around our body, we can feel an energetic shift taking place. I intended to wield the sword around my grandfather's body to help free him so he could go into higher octaves of light. My only concern was how to do this spiritual work incognito.

After daybreak, I drove to the hospital, long before visiting hours, and sneaked into my grandfather's room unannounced. I was sure to find only a corpse. Instead, to my great surprise, he was sitting up in a chair and had eaten breakfast for the first time in days.

"What are you doing here so early?" he asked me.

"I thought you would be dead," I said sheepishly, quickly hiding my sword.

The rest of the family was amazed at his recovery and told me I had brought him back to life. I knew that it was not me, but the love bond between us and the spiritual work of the angels, in answer to my calls.

We spent time together during the following days walking down the hospital corridor and visiting, until he was able to go home. We had a last meal together and he still enjoyed his red wine. Then, he told me this would be my last trip to see him and I dismissed his foreboding with levity.

A year later, I received a phone call that he had passed away, three weeks before Christmas. I was stunned by the intensity of the grief I felt, and the pain of separation, especially since I had lived thousands of miles away from him for many years already. Now, it seemed like there was no time or space, only the pain of separation.

I ran into Elizabeth Clare Prophet at a Christmas party and told her what had happened. She gently rubbed my back while we sang carols together, until all of the pain I had been carrying was dissolved. A couple of days later, I ran into her again and she told me that she had been watching my grandfather's transition. She said he was shooting up like a rocket, from octave to octave in the heaven-world, which put my heart to rest.

I was married the following year, December 1998, and burned a candle for my grandfather at the wedding. I could feel his presence there. Then within three months, I became pregnant. I conceived on Wesak, the day of the festival of the buddhas, when we celebrate the birth and enlightenment of Gautama.

Upon awakening I saw my causal body. Behind it was merging another causal body of great beauty, which I later understood to belong to my unborn child.

That Wesak afternoon, I visited a dear friend, Dr. Elisabeth Caspari, who was a friend and colleague of Dr. Maria Montessori. Mother Caspari was almost one hundred years old and loved to speak French, the language of her childhood in the Swiss Alps. She had worked with children and educators all over the world, promulgating the educational methods that Maria Montessori had imparted to her when the two had lived in India during World War II. Mother Caspari was very devout, as was Dr. Maria

Montessori. Mother Caspari told me that the two of them had nurtured a strong tie to Mother Mary and had studied and practiced Theosophy.

Now, Mother Caspari lived in a small village above Emigrant, Montana where she had moved to help Elizabeth Clare Prophet develop Montessori International, a school for children of spiritual seekers with a mission to offer the most effective and inspiring educational methods.

Her only conversation with me on this visit was about souls coming in from higher octaves of light. I told her I was not ready to have children yet, and she dismissed my protest. She insisted that they were coming, because "The child," she said, as the masters in the East had taught her, "chooses the mother."

Mother Caspari also confided to me that in a past life, she bore the same name, Elisabeth, and was the cousin of Mary. She said my visit reminded her of the time when Mary had visited Elisabeth and the baby John had leaped in her womb.

A month later when my pregnancy was confirmed, I realized that Mother Caspari had been tuning into the conception of my child. Several dreams showed me this was the soul of my grandfather, coming back as a little girl.

My daughter was born in January of the year 2000. The first year of her life, the similarities between her unconscious expressions and his, from the way he would eat, to the way in which he walked, to his fiery determination and willpower, were downright amazing.

As my daughter's new personality settled in, these similarities became less apparent, but during the first two years of life, the transition between the two lifetimes was clearly noticeable to me.

Auld Lang Syne

I will never forget July 2006. I had been attending a session of Summit University in San Diego. The day after the session was my birthday and my friends threw a party for me on the beach. I was especially excited, and so were they, because Mother was coming.

We had a wonderful time. We jumped in the waves together, talked and ate, and huddled together around a bonfire like giggling teenagers. It was so much fun and Mother was right there with us.

Then, in a moment of reflection, Mother told me that she had prayed to El Morya to help her to heal her inner child and to process the pain of being "left out" in her youth. She told me that hanging out with us that night had been the answer to her prayer.

At one point, we had just run back in from the waves and Mother stood and held both of my hands, and we deeply smiled at each other. I felt such an incredible outpouring of joy and love. It seemed like all time had stopped.

Later, when it was time to go, Mother started to walk back to the vacation home in which she stayed. As she turned around to wave at us one last time, I started to sing Auld Lang Syne and everyone joined in.

> "Should auld acquaintance be forgot,
> and never brought to mind?
> Should auld acquaintance be forgot
> and days of auld lang syne?
>
> For auld lang syne, my dear,
> For auld lang syne,
> We'll take a cup o' kindness yet
> For auld lang syne."

Little did we know then that only a few years later, we would no longer see her like this. Such an outcome was beyond our wildest imagination.

The servant leader

In the summer of 1996, I joined the staff of The Summit Lighthouse. Mother had hired Belgian business leader Gilbert Cleirbaut to help restructure the organization. An avid reader of Peter Senge, Gilbert was an expert in organizational reengineering, helping companies become more efficient at reaching their goals. Gilbert's job was to help The Summit Lighthouse move into a new cycle of development, and dictations from the ascended masters had emphasized the importance of his work.

Gilbert and I had a good rapport and often would see eye to eye. I loved his frankness and his heart of gold. He loved to "call a spade a spade," as he said, even with the media, which offended the entrenched powerbrokers of the organization. "If you don't want to be perceived as a cult, you have to stop behaving like one," he would say as he introduced new paradigms that would become essential to meet the growing needs of spiritual seekers in the twenty-first century.

I was in charge of publishing the organizational newsletter, *Heart to Heart,* and later, the annual report. My job was to share with the larger community Mother and Gilbert's most recent attempts to move the church into a learning and loving culture.

Building a Culture of Love was the title of a booklet that Gilbert had written upon arrival, having assessed the weaknesses in the movement at the time.

Even though the organization had many well-meaning and loving people, it had become quite insular in a number of ways, crippled by an unchallenged, authoritarian, top-down leadership based on hierarchical orthodoxy. This mindset, while comfortable for some, was creating a dichotomy within the movement. Self-examination was the need of the hour. A deep shift had to be made. Gilbert even introduced "360-degree feedback," a horizontal management tool where everyone gives feedback to everyone else, irrespective of place or position.

I would visit Gilbert downstairs in the little blue house which was the Office of the President, and from where we admired the snows of Electric Peak. I could feel a wall of light, of spiritual protection and sponsorship, as I walked through the door, which he often left open to reinforce the message of openness that he was trying to instill.

After giving his all for about four years, Gilbert ultimately resigned under great pressure. A few months before his orchestrated removal, he shared with our team a puzzling incident. Late one night, Mother had come to his doorstep unannounced with an urgent message: "That which they are doing to me they will also do to you," was what she had foreseen.

Many of the people who had shown enthusiasm for Gilbert were ousted as well. It was a very sad time, a setback in both Mother and the masters' attempt to enfire the movement with a new thrust based on truth, good will and personal accountability. The only silver lining to this cloud was the message Gilbert had engraved upon the hearts of those who would receive it: servant leadership.

"Before you are fit to lead another," he would say, "you must be willing to wash their feet, like Jesus." This he taught to those working closely with him, including Mother. This he taught not so much by word but by example.

Gilbert was as "harmless as doves." His undoing was that he was not as "wise as serpents," an essential quality for sorting out the darker side of human ambition.

As the years and cycles move on, there are hopeful signs that the community is recovering. More and more, people are learning to express good will toward one another's efforts and viewpoints, and this realization is, slowly but surely, mending the rifts.

Though at times it has appeared that we are journeying down separate, but nonetheless parallel rivers, let us remember the great confluence that is to come. Having been tried by the fire of our seeming contradictions, our dedication to the cause of Light will prevail and see us through.

The gift of the Guru

One summer day, I went up to visit Mother with a friend. Mother sat us down on her pastel flowered couch and served us watermelon.

I didn't know what to do. Watermelon was the one food I absolutely couldn't stand eating, but my higher self was reminding me never to refuse what the guru brings. Mother came back into the room and gave me the biggest piece. I gulped, and started to cut away at the pink crispness with my spoon. Slowly, I put the fruit into my mouth and began to chew. It was an interesting experiment. Instead of gagging, which is what I usually do when I have watermelon in my mouth, I was able to eat the whole thing.

The next summer when I was sitting around a table with Mother, it was at a restaurant in the San Diego Aquarium. There, Mother decided that everyone at her table should eat ice cream. I was surprised. For years, I had been following a strict whole food diet encouraged by the masters that did not include sugar. What was Mother up to, I wondered? I had taken pride in my unblemished dietary discipline. I began licking the cone and sure enough, it tasted sweet. Moreover, I did not reel from it and I realized that eating ice cream would be okay from time to time.

Mother was teaching me not to be rigid or fanatic. She was showing me the difference between the "letter of the law" and the "spirit of the law," which is love.

Yellow bottles

One day, I was sitting in Mother's living room admiring the multicolored glass bottles in her window, through which sunlight gently shone. I noticed that the bottles were every color of the causal body except yellow, so I determined to find some yellow bottles for her.

The following year, a few days before Mother's birthday, I stumbled upon two yellow glass bottles in the bottom rack of a store in Livingston and brought them to her in a yellow gift bag. She was thrilled and couldn't stop talking about the yellow bottles. Now, her collection was complete, with the seven rainbow rays.

I understood in that moment that the best gift was always to supply the difference, to see what someone lacked and to bring it forth.

O Christmas tree

A couple of weeks before Christmas 1997, Mother had stopped by our office. With childlike enthusiasm, she told us how much she liked her Christmas tree that year. One of the men on staff had gone up in the woods to cut it down for her and she said she had never seen a tree that big.

Before leaving, she invited us to come up to her house to see the tree, but no one took her up on the offer, except me. After work that evening, I drove up the winding road to her home and rang the doorbell. One of her attendants greeted me. Then Mother came out and ushered me into the living room where the tree was erected. It was a magnificent spruce tree with wide, generous branches, so tall that the top was cut off. On each branch hung a vast array of beautiful ornaments, which had probably come from students all over the world. In the middle shone strands of multicolored rainbow lights.

Mother and I talked for a few minutes, and then she told me it was time for her to put her youngest son Seth to bed. She asked me to stay in her living room while she went to his bedroom to read him a story.

I sat down on the floor and waited for her, gazing up at the tree, which the masters have said is a symbol of our causal body. As I sat there in silent communion, I felt Mother's presence come upon me so strongly. Her light essence was such that I could hardly move. I was glued to the ground. Then, a while later, Mother came back into the room and it was time for me to leave. The spiritual work had been accomplished.

Spiritual mantles

Spiritual mantles are like layers of spiritual protection, attainment and connectedness to the heaven-world. The masters have taught that everyone has a mantle, which is the mantle of our own Mighty I AM Presence and Holy Christ Self. An ascended master can also place a mantle of their choosing on someone for a particular service to render. In the case of Mother, there were a number of mantles that the masters had bestowed upon her over the years. These allowed her to perform all kinds of blessings and healings.

A few months before Mother retired, I had seen a number of memos circulating around the Office of the President. They were surmising which appointed successor would inherit Mother's mantles. This burdened me, so I went to visit Dorothy Lee Fulton, a friend who had more contact with Mother than I did. "Do you think you could let Mother know what is going on?" I asked.

At that very moment, Mother waltzed in through the door, unannounced. "Therese has something important to tell you," Dorothy Lee told Mother.

I proceeded to explain what I had seen and heard about the mantle debate. Mother was astonished. It seemed unfathomable to her that people would want to take something that is only God's to give.

The resonance of her voice shifted, in a similar way to

what had happened during my baptism. It seemed to be coming from her Mighty I AM Presence. "Don't they realize," she said "that I have trained for this for aeons?"

Having said that, her voice returned to its normal chirpy state and she told us she would be off to have lunch, most probably with some of the very people whose names were on the memos.

One of the most important mantles Mother had received was from Saint Germain. Through this mantle, Mother had an additional spiritual protection that allowed her to take dictations from the higher mental plane of the Christ mind without interference from the astral plane. This preserved the purity of the release of light and also afforded a high degree of accuracy in relaying the masters' messages, which were later printed in *Pearls of Wisdom*.

Brian and I attended Mother's last dictation, in 1999, which was to be from Gautama Buddha. We witnessed how she struggled with the fact that, like never before, the dictation was not taking place. She pleaded for the master to come, and eventually, Saint Germain came instead. It would have been easy at that point for Mother to start channeling the astral plane. Other messengers had done this before her in their latter years, including Geraldine Innocente in the Bridge to Freedom and Edna Ballard in the I AM Movement. Mother did not. She would not settle for anything less than the highest vibration, even if it cost her her reputation.

Mother was very humble about her situation. She was willing to consider that, perhaps, the masters had now chosen someone else to give dictations and she was willing, not only to surrender her role, but also to support a new messenger if that messenger was forthcoming.

New "messengers" had started to crop up. First came Monroe and Carolyn Shearer, who had once worked alongside Mark and Mother, and had moved on to start the Temple of the Presence. Then, a few years later came David Lewis, another longtime church member, who started the Heart Center, as well as others.

Members left in droves to follow these new "messengers." When the Shearers started their movement, they sent flyers promoting their events, as well as an audio recording of a dictation from Carolyn, to everyone on the church's mailing list. As I examined the work of all of these new messengers, I would feel a dull, unsettling and even painful sensation in my chakras, something I generally experience around psychic energies. I didn't want anything to do with it.

Mother was more openminded. She ask me to lend her my copy of the Shearers' CD so she could listen to it. I could tell that she was coming from a place of goodwill, regardless of any personal differences that had come up between her and the Shearers in the past. A few days later she gave the CD back to me.

"What did you think of it, Mother?" I asked.

"It's psychic," she said with a shrug. It almost seemed as if she had been disappointed that it was not the real thing.

The master Morya said, "If the messenger be an ant, heed him." What he meant was that we must respect ourselves enough to respect the message of God in others, and to heed that message when it is confirmed by our own conscience. We must not, however, look for someone to take on the role of our spiritual decision-making. This places a burden upon them that they should not have to bear. We must look to our own evolving understanding.

God gave us free will to make choices for ourselves. We cannot wait to be told what to do at every turn. When we seek to follow direction from an "authority" out there, we abdicate our free will, and then when things go wrong, we blame the authority and renounce our responsibility. The masters want us to exercise our own discernment and judgment in any given situation, and then come up with an action plan. In so doing, we earn the good karma of co-creating with God, and not simply one of obedience.

Free will is what makes us God, a gift even angels do not earn until they reach the archangelic level. The opportunity to co-create with God's energy is a tremendous blessing. Gautama Buddha said that you cannot co-create with God in the absence of good will. When we earnestly "TRY," which Mark Prophet taught is an acronym for "Theos Rules You," we engage in the fullness of our divine destiny. We reap the fruits of ingenuity and good will that we have sown.

Mother stopped giving dictations in 1999. Between 1964 and 1999, she received nearly 4000 dictations, an incredible feat for any one person. These dictations are spiritual tools that transcend time and space. The masters' light essence flows through the recordings and you experience their vibration, teaching and blessings, goading you on towards an individualized expression of co-creativity and union with God.

Messenger of Music

During the winter of 1995, I had seen Dorothy Lee Fulton in the chapel. I knew that she had written many ethereal songs for the masters and that she was a chela of Mother Mary. I thought it would be interesting to meet her, but there had not been any opportunity to do so.

Then one night in 1996, we met in a dream. A couple of days later, I drove to the town of Gardiner to make a bank deposit and as I was walking out of the building, we practically bumped into each other. Dorothy Lee said, "Hello," like we already knew each other, and asked me to come see her.

I started to visit Dorothy Lee more often and she taught me many things about God. Dorothy Lee, who was Brahms in a past life, had been composing since her earliest childhood. She shared with me that no one had taught her how to play piano. She instinctively knew.

Now, Dorothy Lee was receiving songs directly from the ascended masters. Mother Mary had placed upon her the mantle of Messenger of Music, with which she could tune into the etheric plane by the power of the Holy Spirit. It was awesome to hold the pages on which these notes and words were written. There was so much light in them.

Dorothy Lee also taught me how to play canasta and we played cards together with other friends, often interrupted by the energy of a master coming through. It would expand her throat chakra so quickly that she would have to cough every time.

Dorothy Lee coached and comforted me on my spiritual path, and taught me how to see the rainbows around lights. Then, one day, she needed to move out of her apartment, so we rented a house together with a couple of other ladies. We were roommates until my wedding, and I stayed in a little tower room, under the roof, that overlooked the whole valley. It was quite magical.

On the night of our wedding, Brian and I drove off to a nearby resort, where we had made reservations. Much to our surprise, there were only smoking rooms left so we decided to head back to the house, in the tower room, under the stars. It was a funny sight to see us come back in the door on our wedding night, but we all felt like family, so it was no big deal.

Dorothy Lee and I shared many special and intimate moments together, and often talked about life on the other side. She helped me to publish my book, *The Legend of the Ancient of Days*, as a gift from Mother Mary. Then came time for me to help her publish her memoirs, entitled *Here I AM*. She also kept encouraging me to write down my stories, before I even knew I would.

A marriage made in heaven

I met Brian through a mutual friend. I started to visit him in 1996 for personal coaching and counseling. I noticed that when I was around him, my soul would leap for joy. Then, for about six months, I discontinued counseling and would only talk on the phone from time to time just to keep in touch.

One Sunday in the spring of 1998, I heard my higher self saying, "Go to Bozeman. Go see Brian." I got in the car and drove the hour to Brian's little apartment, in answer to divine order. It felt somewhat awkward knocking on the door in the middle of the afternoon, unannounced, not quite sure why I was there. When Brian opened the door, I asked him if he would like to go see a movie, which was the first thing that came out of my mouth. Brian didn't seem surprised and I felt relieved. He told me to come back a little later.

The movie was called "Deep Impact," appropriately so. As we watched, Brian put his arm around my chair without second thought and I felt the most powerful spiritual energy coming over us, like a shower of light. I had never experienced this with someone before, especially in a movie theater, and knew it was significant. The next day, I shared this with Brian and we decided to meet again the following weekend for an official "date."

The date turned out to be disastrous. Everything

seemed to go wrong. We experienced a lot of "opposition," the negative energy sent from the force of darkness on the astral plane that makes things go awry, to counter the positive potential of a given moment. Still, we decided to brave it one more time so I came over to his apartment a week later.

We ordered Chinese food and started to watch a video, sitting opposite each other on the couch. Only our feet were touching. Stronger and stronger, unbeknownst to Brian, I felt a strong figure-eight flow of spiritual light between us, an energetic reciprocity that from Alpha to Omega, and from Omega back to Alpha. My body was filled with such a rush of joy that I didn't know what to make of it. When I went home that night, I could not sleep for hours.

In the weeks that followed, I asked Brian if he would go to a conference in San Diego where I was working. He agreed, which made me really happy. One late morning there, I ran into him in the lobby of the hotel where everyone was staying. I felt the unusual urge to go down to Mission Beach with him, but since it was the middle of the workday, I asked if he would drive me to purchase some film for my camera instead.

"Sure," he said. "Where do you want to go?"

"There's a place I know next to Mission Beach that sells film," I replied.

"Okay," he said, and we were off. We drove across town. Then when we got to the beach, I asked him if he would walk down the shoreline with me. A couple of hundred yards later was Mother, sitting on the sand! She beamed a great big smile, like she was expecting us. "I was wondering when the two of you were going to get together,"she said, much to our surprise. Then we sat down together and had a wonderful talk.

A few months later, while I was visiting my family in Vermont, Brian and I got engaged over the phone. Then, I left for a conference in Ottawa, my head spinning with a thousand joys and concerns.

When I told the friend I was staying with that we had just gotten engaged, she pulled a wedding dress out of her closet. It was beautiful and fit me perfectly, so she told me to take it home. Here, with heaven's help, was a wedding dress dropping into my lap two days after our engagement!

One night, Brian and I had just had an argument and I started to question our commitment. I told Brian I wanted to go to the Bozeman Hot Springs, even though the facility would be closing in about thirty minutes. I knew I just had to go.

Still grumpy, we walked into the pools, only to find Mother smiling at us. Then, in the dressing room, she asked me if we had picked a wedding date. "No, Mother," I said. "We've been looking at the astrology and there are no good dates."

"Pick the worst date you can find," she said. "Then I won't have to hold the balance for you." That was quite an answer. As I reflected more upon what Mother was telling us, I realized that even though astrology can be a helpful tool, we must not become slaves to it.

Next, Mother asked, "Do you know where you will get married?" I told her of Inspiration Point, a tiny chapel overlooking the Yellowstone River. "No," she said, "you must be married in King Arthur's Court," referring to the largest building at the Royal Teton Ranch. "I want to be there and I want to bless you."

I told Brian about my conversation with Mother and we decided to look for the best of the worst dates available. A few weeks later, I ran into Mother at a restaurant and told her we finally had a date, which made her very happy.

Still, I had doubts and concerns. As the wedding approached, these did not let up and I shared my anxiety with Mother during a luncheon. "Why?" she asked, with the biggest smile, and I could not explain.

On the day of my wedding, as I stood outside the chapel waiting for my turn to go in, I was so terrified I thought I might pass out. Again, Mother came up to me and cheered me, encouraging me forward. It was such a momentous time, such an initiation to pass, so different from the carefree preparations of my first marriage.

During the wedding ceremony, a tremendous blessing of spiritual energy descended. We were filled with light to where we could hardly touch the ground! Later during the reception, Mother was sitting next to me and I put my head on her shoulder. Mother said there was so much love in the room. Then, she said tenderly, "I am devoted to you for life." I felt deeply moved. "Yes, Mother," I replied, "I am devoted to you for life too, and I know I have been for many lifetimes."

A year or so later, I visited with Mother again and she reiterated how grateful she was that Brian and I had come together. Looking back, I can see how this marriage has brought incredible growth for the both of us, though it is not an easy path. Time after time, as the limits of our personal expectations are stretched through ups and downs, the words on Mother's wedding card to us ring truer than ever:

> "Have patience and understanding
> Hold each other always in high esteem
> Have a sense of humor
> Hold onto your dreams
> Have respect for one another
> Hold each other forever in your hearts."

Reverse the tide

During the summer of 1998, Brian, some friends and I headed for the beach to make a bonfire party like we had enjoyed the previous year with Mother. It was my birthday again. The fire was going and all of the food was out, when the tide started to come in. The beach was beginning to be swamped. Towels were getting soaked and the water came up to the fire. Our party was about to be spoiled!

I got up and made a prayer to Lanello, who is a master of the elements, to reverse the tide so that our party would not be ruined. Then I started doing "reverse the tide" decrees, a prayer, originally given by the ascended master El Morya for the reversing of the tide of darkness on the planet.

The others joined in, in a joking manner. This seemed a little out of the ordinary, but I was enthusiastic, and since it was my birthday, why not give it a shot?

After the decrees, we continued our party and a little while later, we noticed the water line. It was farther up than us on both sides of the beach, yet had circumvented our fire. We were the only ones left in the sand at that level. We gave thanks to God and enjoyed the rest of the evening.

We should never underestimate the power of the spoken word. The Bible says, "Thou shalt decree a thing and it shall be established unto thee." When we engage our free will through the power of sound, we harness the power of creation, the "word in the beginning," and we can work miracles.

The second coming

The secret chamber of the heart is an inner sanctuary where our soul connects to our Christ Self. It is also the eight-petaled eighth chakra. Saint Teresa of Avila called it the "interior castle."

On Easter Sunday of 2001, as I was meditating on the master Jesus, I saw with my inner sight this secret chamber as a beautiful stone chapel with gothic spirals overlooking a lake, and surrounded by woods and flowers. It somehow reminded me of the days of King Arthur.

Into this chapel came Jesus as the representative of my Christ Self and we practiced the ritual of the alchemical marriage. It was so uplifting and comforting to know that we have this place inside our being where we can meet God face-to-face.

During this cosmic interlude, I was shown that many souls who had been with Jesus reincarnated over and over again during the last two thousand years to follow in his footsteps and to further his teachings. They would become the instrument of his "second coming," and the Christ consciousness in them would now bless and heal the world. This, the apostle Paul had alluded to when he said, "Let that mind be in you that was also in Christ Jesus."

I wrote a poem to describe the glyph I had received. It is called "The Promise," and describes the bond of love between Jesus and his followers that has held strong throughout the centuries.

I come from a very Christian family and have had many encounters with Christians. Some believe that the teachings given through Theosophy and the ascended masters cannot be reconciled with their traditional faith. How can you, for instance, show an appreciation for Buddha and Shiva, and still accept Jesus as your Lord and Savior?

We are at a new nexus in time and space, the beginning of the Age of Aquarius. The teachings brought forth by Jesus and disseminated by his apostles set a foundation for the previous age, which was the age of Pisces.

During the Piscean age, while many of Jesus' teachings made it into mainstream Christianity, others did not, including his more esoteric teachings. These he shared with the Essene community in Palestine, as well as in his journey to India during the "lost years," where he was known as Issa.

On one of my visits to see Mother Caspari, she shared with me that as a young adult, she had travelled to the East with a friend. They had taken the ancient caravan route and had stopped at a monastery in Ladakh along the way. While they were admiring the view from the roof top, the monastery librarian and two other monks reverently handed the ladies a parchment scroll. The scroll was held between two wooden slabs and wrapped in colorful brocades. "These books say your Jesus was here," the monks told her. Greatly moved, Mother Caspari remembered the scripture in the Gospel of John, "But there are also many other things which Jesus did, were every one of them to be written, I suppose that the world itself could not contain the books that would be written."

Some of Jesus' teachings were not acceptable to the religious power elite of the third century, who codified the Christian creed during the Nicean Council. All of the beliefs of the time were reassessed through the lens of ecclesiatic authority for hegemonic purposes. Church fathers even went so far as to hold a debate over whether women had souls, and the camp favoring women won by only one vote.

Many of these church fathers were fallen angels, who had gravitated to a place of authority, and wielded that authority to conform Jesus' legacy to their own prejudices. Any text or tradition attributed to Jesus that sustained a belief in reincarnation, or in a personal divinity outside of Jesus, had to be reframed, undermined, excluded from the biblical canon, or eliminated altogether. Gnostics were viciously eradicated in the fanatic and bloody debacle that ensued, books were burned or buried, and all beliefs outside the new "norm" were proclaimed heresy, even if they had originated in Jesus himself.

The fallen ones have an innate hatred of Christ and cannot embrace the promise of personal Christhood. They refuse to serve Christ as a seed potential in man and resent the fact that man, who was made a little lower than the angels, can become crowned with greater glory by becoming Christ, as the Book of Hebrews foretells.

They seek to curtail mankind's spiritual growth by holding hostage the true teaching. They indoctrinate people into worshiping the personage of Jesus as an only Son of God, instead of modeling the Christ consciousness that he represents, which is the true "only begotten Son."

Long ago, they relinquished their divine potential to play out their pride, egotism and rebellion. Having severed their tie to God, they can no longer receive the light descending from above as co-creative potential. Instead, they feast on light stolen from unsuspecting souls. This happens every time people engage in activities that tie you to the astral plane and syphon the light of the chakras, including the "sex, drugs, and rock and roll" culture that emerged in the 1960s.

Having made boatloads of negative karma, the fallen ones resist the immutable law of karma and reincarnation, "as you sow, so shall you reap." They become experts at dodging negative returning karma and at enticing others to shoulder that karma. They do this by steering mankind's free will towards idolatrous relationships, binding associations and karmic entanglements with them that, lifetime after lifetime, become most difficult to disengage from.

"But woe to you," Jesus exposed. "Because you shut off the kingdom of heaven from people. For you do not enter in yourselves, nor do you allow those who are entering to go in."

Today, we have entered the Age of Aquarius and there is a step-up of spiritual energies. The new dispensation is for every Son and Daughter of God to become the Christ, as Jesus and other masters have demonstrated. "The work that I do, ye shall do," said Jesus, "and greater works than these shall you do, because I go unto my Father."

The Promise

Was I not with you, Master
When you made the blind man see
And broke the bread in morsels
On the shores of Galilee?

Did we not linger on the beach
After the multitudes heard you speak
Thirsting for the living water
You promised we would drink?

My head upon your shoulder
Your heartbeat close to mine
Your hand upon my forehead
Our union was divine.

"Wait for me," you said to me
Looking at the sands of time,
"Watch and pray for me each day
Forever you'll be mine."

I watched them nail you to the tree
And tear your garments into shreds,
I prayed while you were in the tomb
I hoped you were not dead.

I ran to you on Easter morn
I was so overwhelmed,
I couldn't contain the joy to know
You were with us once again!

At eternity you seemed to gaze
With essence from above,
"Wait for me," you said again.
"Watch and pray, my love."

I watched the world around me change
Two thousand years I prayed
I knew that you would come again,
That things wouldn't be the same.

Longing for your heartbeat
And for your hand in mine,
I didn't forget your loving words
Across the sands of time.

Now lately when I think of you
I feel your breath in me
Not since that day upon the shore
Have I felt you so near.

Your hand upon my forehead
Your heartbeat close to mine,
You live inside me, Lord, each day
Forever you'll be mine.

Mother Mary in a suit

In November 2001, I was in labor with my second child, hoping for the best, since the delivery of my first daughter had been most difficult. Between contractions, I prayed to Mother Mary as the hours went by, offering an Aquarian version of the classic prayer that she gave to Elizabeth Clare Prophet.

> "Hail Mary, full of grace, the Lord is with thee
> Blessed art thou among women and
> blessed is the fruit of thy womb, Jesus.
> Holy Mary, Mother of God,
> Pray for us, Sons and Daughters of God,
> Now and at the hour of our victory
> over sin, disease and death."

When the contractions became very close, my husband and I drove to the hospital, which was only a few blocks away. I went into a hot tub in the delivery room, and a couple of hours later, the pain was so intense I could no longer tolerate it.

All of a sudden, Mother Mary appeared before me, dressed in a cream-colored business suit, with a briefcase in her hand and high heel pumps. I had never imagined Mother Mary in such a way, because I had always visualized her in gown and veil. I guess she meant business!

Seeing her helped me to calm down. I knew that as long as she was with me, no harm would come to me or to my child. The pain did not lessen, and as my cervix continued to open, Mother Mary gave me the visualization of the twelve starry focal points in a circle. My cervix had become the twelve starry focal points and my child's head was going to crown through. A short time later, my second daughter was born.

The psychology of success

I still remember the joy, sitting in the church of Saint Francis in Salta, Argentina, reciting a prayer from the ascended master Kuthumi, who was embodied as Saint Francis. This prayer, I found out later, had been published by The Summit Lighthouse and set to music by Dorothy Lee Fulton. It is a beautiful testament to the spiritual path.

"I AM Light
Glowing Light, radiating Light, intensified Light!
God consumes my darkness,
Transmuting it into Light.
This day I AM a focus of the Central Sun.
Flowing through me is a crystal river,
A living fountain of Light
That can never be qualified
by human thought and feeling.
I AM an outpost of the divine
Such darkness as has used me is swallowed up
by the mighty river of Light which I AM.
I AM, I AM, I AM Light!
I live, I live, I live in Light.
I AM light's fullest dimension
I AM Light's purest intention.
I AM Light, Light, Light!
Flooding the world everywhere I move,
Blessing, strengthening and conveying
The purpose of the kingdom of heaven."

Kuthumi is the master psychologist. He helps us to overcome our deepest emotional blocks and issues. He strives to unfold a more comprehensive understanding of the human "psyche," which in Greek means "soul." All enlightened psychological pursuits that he sponsors lead to soul awakening and soul freedom.

I could sense Kuthumi's guiding hand behind the work that Brian and Caroline Hanstke had developed to counsel people, like The Inner Family Archetype Model. Now, I was working with these concepts as well.

The inner family archetypes act as transformers of the divine energy of Father, Mother, Christ and Holy Spirit in our everyday lives. When we understand how these archetypes operate, for better or for worse, we can transcend unloving, self-limiting habits locked within our personality and childhood training.

In 2001, after many months, we published the book *Why We Do What We Do: Four Pathways to Your Authentic Self*, which describes how the inner family archetypes influence our thoughts, feelings and relationships. It was during this time that I woke up one morning from a vivid dream. I was standing under a statue of Saint Francis that had come to life, and the master was telling me that the inner family archetype work was key to my ascension.

Then in 2003, I was working on a sequel to the book when I had another dream. Before me stood three masters dressed in Franciscan robes. I knew them to be El Morya, Kuthumi and Djwal Kul. Kuthumi was in the center and handed me a giant book, bound in brown leather. Across it was a title, embossed in letters of gold: *The Psychology of Success*. This became the title of our second book.

The book that I received on the inner was much larger than what we had published at the time. Looking back, I know that the meaning of this dream and the wisdom contained within that volume will continue to unfold, as we open our hearts to receive the golden age psychology that the masters teach at night in the retreats.

Saying goodbye

I loved my paternal grandmother dearly, whom we affectionately called Memere. I had spent several years of my childhood living with my grandparents and the bond of affection that was created never diminished.

Now, in the winter of 2002, Memere was in her nineties, laying in a nursing home in Chantilly, France. Her right leg had been amputated because of gangrene.

A few days earlier, I had spoken to her over the telephone as she was being wheeled off to the operating room and she told me how concerned she was that she might not come back. Her birthday was right around the corner, and I assured her that she would come out of the operation so that we could celebrate! Since Memere had made it through the operation, it was time for me to fulfill that promise. I left my daughters with Brian and got on a plane.

I spent several days by Memere's side, and I washed her hair and painted her nails, as in old times. She was not recuperating well and I realized this would be our last visit. When I returned home, I told Brian it seemed Memere had survived the operation only long enough to say good-bye.

Memere was apprehensive about death. Brian understood this, and told me that in his communion with Kuthumi, he was shown that the master would come at the time of her transition. This gave me comfort and several days later, we received a phone call that Memere had passed away.

That night, Brian saw Memere on inner planes, but she did not recognize him or Kuthumi. She was bewildered and confused, until Mother Mary came to greet her.

Brian explained that a few hours before passing, Memere had recited the Hail Mary, which opened her consciousness to receive Mother Mary. Once this contact with an ascended being was established, she was able to recognize Kuthumi, and even to see Brian.

I learned from this experience that our consciousness determines what takes place after we pass on. We can only see and go where our free will consents.

As I meditated on Memere's transition, the hymn of "The Lost Chord" resonated through me. How often had Memere, as a professional pianist, sat at the keyboard. Now, in her time of transition, the Hail Mary had become the lost chord that would usher her soul to higher octaves of light.

The Lost Chord

Seated one day at the organ,
I was weary and ill at ease,
And my fingers wandered idly
Over the noisy keys;
I know not what I was playing,
Or what I was dreaming then,
But I struck one chord of music,
Like the sound of a great Amen,
Like the sound of a great Amen.

It flooded the crimson twilight,
Like the close of an angel's psalm,
And it lay on my fevered spirit,
With a touch of infinite calm,
It quieted pain and sorrow,
Like love overcoming strife,
It seemed the harmonious echo
From our discordant life,
It linked all the perplexed meanings
Into one perfect peace,
And trembled away into silence,
As if it were loth to cease;
I have sought but I seek it vainly,
That one lost chord divine,
Which came from the soul of the organ,
And entered into mine.

It may be that death's bright angel
 Will speak in that chord again;
 It may be that only in Heav'n
 I shall hear that great Amen.
It may be that death's bright angel
 Will speak in that chord again;
 It may be that only in Heav'n
 I shall hear that great Amen.

Adelaide Procter (1825-1864)

Parlez moi d'amour

One afternoon, not long after Memere passed away, a friend called to say that Mother Caspari was close to making her transition. I jumped in the car and drove to her home. Only a caregiver was there so I had the opportunity to go into her bedroom, where she was laying. I could tell she was in a lot of discomfort, both physically and emotionally.

It was surprising to me that someone as close to God as Mother Caspari could experience such unrest as she neared her transition. She was longing for comfort, so I took her hand. I started to sing to her in French, as we had done together in the past. It seemed like I was rocking her inner child with these songs of her childhood in the Swiss Alps, songs of love and songs of worship.

> "Parlez moi d'amour,
> Redites moi des choses tendres…"

With each song, she seemed to relax a little more. She could not speak or open her eyes, but she clasped my hand tightly. Then, I put a few drops of holy water that I had brought with me into her mouth and she yearned for more.

I continued to sing and to give her holy water until she was calm and I knew that it was time to go. When I returned home, the phone rang. Mother Caspari had just passed away.

I will never forget this holy and somber moment, standing on the edge of two worlds. I could see that sometimes, the closer we are to God, the more challenging the initiation. Jesus experienced this on the cross when he said, "My God, my God, why hast thou forsaken me?"

In the days that followed, I felt the great, great joy of Mother Caspari's soul, like a beaming sunshine, blessing us all. She had won the victory, like Jesus, who went on to affirm, "It is finished. Done with this episode in strife, I AM made one with eternal life."

Please come into my heart

The Maha Chohan is a master who is the representative of the Holy Spirit. He is both very stern and very loving. We keep a portrait of him in almost every room and his eyes seem to be watching us at all times, with interest, care and concern.

Driving home one sunny Sunday afternoon, my spirits were low. I felt bereft and disconnected from God, so I started to speak to the Maha Chohan. Between tears, I told him that I needed his presence with me and begged him to come whenever I would say the words, "Beloved Maha Chohan, please come into my heart."

Since that afternoon, I have made this call, "Beloved Maha Chohan, please come into my heart," almost daily and sometimes, several times a day. Each time, I feel his response as a burst of spiritual fire within the flame inside my heart. It is a tangible expansion of light that comes up from my heart into my head area, both strong and gentle. The call works unfailingly to remind me that he is always with me.

The masters have told us that the call compels the answer. They want us to connect with them, using our free will, and it can be as simple as these five words, "Please come into my heart."

Lanello

I love the ascended master Lanello deeply. Though I did not know him when he was Mark Prophet, I feel very close to him in his ascended state.

Years ago, Lanello gave a dictation in which he asked us to solicit his help concerning whatever problems we might be having. He asked us to write a letter addressed to him and burn it, so the angels can take the energy into the higher octaves.

I have written to Lanello countless times about every situation imaginable, from little problems to major ordeals. Each time, the situation has cleared up. It is astounding how involved he can be with our day-to-day problems, no matter how small.

Once, I was standing in the chapel, communing with Lanello and thinking about the rose flower, which is also my middle name. I heard Lanello, plain as day. "Yes, you are a rose," he said, "and we are going to remove your thorns!"

On another occasion I remember visiting Lanello's retreat over the Rhein Valley in my etheric body at night. I can still see the towers spiraling above the retreat and the huge library room with a great big fireplace, where the students gather.

Then one morning, while I was vacationing in Hawaii, I woke up remembering Lanello's words reminding me that we had spent many lifetimes together, and I knew, in my heart of hearts, that this was true.

Love conquers fear

Elemental essence imbues every living creature. There are many nature spirits, or elementals, who desire to help us, like the gnomes of the earth, the sylphs of the air, the undines of the water and the salamanders of the fire element.

I never felt the help of elementals so much as when I attended a retreat near Lake Louise in the Canadian Rockies, during the month of August 2004, which was like a summer camp for grown-ups wanting to stretch their limitations.

A little while before attending the retreat, Brian and I had talked about inipis, which are Native American sweat lodges. He described them to me as many people huddled inside a tiny, dark cave or tent, sitting on the mud with hot steam coming in your face. Being claustrophobic, his description turned me off completely.

Unbeknownst to me, the first event of the retreat was an inipi. I could not back down, since I had come to conquer self. I entered the inipi with a lot of apprehension and sure enough, it was like Brian had described. To ward off the sense of panic, I took some deep breaths and started to focus on the fiery rocks in front of me, glowing red in the dark, and the water turning into steam. Then I shut my eyes and prayed while our Native American guide was conducting the ceremony.

In the dark heat, I began to perceive a ruby ray circle with a cross in the middle. At the top of the circle was Sanat Kumara, the ascended master known to the Native Americans as "Great Spirit," "Gitche Manito" and "Wakantanka." I saw Sanat Kumara as the flying eagle at ascension's gate, and all of my fears about the intensity of the ritual dissolved into reverence and bliss.

The following day, we were challenged to walk down thin metal cables that were as high as telephone poles. I was terrified of heights, when all of a sudden, a squirrel came running down the cable, chirping in no ordinary way. He got my attention, and seemed to say, "If I can do it, you can do it." I summoned my courage and went up the post. I knew I had to move from fear to love, so I hugged my teammate, who was just as terrified of this high-wire act as I was. Once our energies shifted, we found the wherewithal to proceed down the cable.

The next exercise was even harder. It involved jumping off a platform higher than trees. As I stood contemplating whether I had the "guts" to do this, a cloud of blue butterflies came fluttering around me, and I had to laugh.

I climbed to the platform, which was no bigger than my two feet, and leaped off. Plummeting downward seemed almost eternal, until the rope attached to my security vest bounced me up and my feet safely touched the ground.

The final challenge was to walk barefoot down fifteen yards of red-hot coals. A Native American spiritual guide called to the elemental spirits from North, South, East and

West for a loving fire and everyone joined him. Later, the staff that was tending the gigantic bonfire and shoveling the hot coals noticed that the flames were burning in the shape of a heart.

I was debating in my mind whether to follow through and looked down. There was a forget-me-not growing at my feet! Forget-me-nots are flowers associated with the master El Morya. Since there was no other flower in sight, I took it as a sign of the master's support.

I removed my shoes to step onto the burning coals and an energy came over my feet like "cosmic galoshes." Walking down the coals, the sensation was purifying and I was neither hurt nor blistered. Then, as my teammates took their turn, I looked up. Shooting stars were flying across the sky.

On this magical night, we broke through barriers of self-limitation and celebrated new levels of empowerment. Cradled by tall, fragrant pine trees under a canopy of sparkling stars, we lost ourselves in the crackling of the roaring bonfire and connected, like never before, to the majestic and most serene presence of God in nature.

The labors of Hercules

Four years after my daughters were born, I started to tune in to the soul of a child who wanted to come into our family. My daughters would often draw pictures that had a baby brother in them. I spent a lot of time getting my body back in optimal health and after several months, became pregnant. This made me very happy.

A couple of months later, I noticed I was bleeding. I prayed to God and to Mother Mary to help me keep the baby. When I went to the hospital for an ultrasound, I knew I would have to let go, but couldn't, as I felt so attached to this child.

Looking at the monitor, I saw there was no sign of life in my womb. I cried and cried. The next day, I passed the fetus and picked it up. It had a head and little stubs for arms and feet. You could even see the definition of a face. The loss that I experienced made me realize just what a miracle life is.

Brian, my daughters and I went up to one of our favorite mountain peaks and had a little cremation service for the baby, asking him to come back if it was God's will. The day was glorious and the spring flowers were blooming on the high alpine meadows. It was still hard to find comfort, but I was starting to let go.

Six months later I became pregnant again. This time, the baby stayed. I could tell it was the same soul and the ultrasound confirmed it was a little boy.

August 2006, it was time to give birth, and the baby was overdue. Two weeks went by and I was being monitored at the hospital several times a day. I didn't want to precipitate the birth. I wanted our child to choose his perfect timing, but I would wake up in the middle of the night with a sense of panic because labor had not started yet.

I spoke to our unborn child and told him I didn't want to mess up his timing. The answer I got back was loud and clear, "Don't worry about the astrology, I need to be born alive!"

Brian and I left for the hospital to induce the birth. When it came time to push, the baby was stuck. One of the nurses was pressing down as hard as she could on my belly while the doctor was using forceps on the baby's head, but my contractions had stopped. I had no strength left to push the baby out.

Then from my mouth came the call, "Hercules!" to the elohim who was embodied as Hercules in Ancient Greece and had performed twelve labors. I knew that the spirit of Hercules could get us out of any tight spot. I had never forgotten the sense of victory standing on top of Mount Half Dome, where the etheric retreat of Hercules is located, after one of the most grueling hikes of my life.

"Hercules," I shouted again, and then the baby popped out.

"These are the labors of Hercules," Brian told the doctor and the nurses standing by, dispelling any sense of strangeness.

My son weighed more than ten pounds and had huge shoulders, wider than his head. He broke his clavicle bone coming out, which healed a few weeks later. How grateful we are that he is here with us, and how thankful to Hercules for getting us through our labors!

The all-seeing eye of God

The elohim are the builders of form and are great beings of light. The elohim Cyclopea focuses the all-seeing eye of God through the third-eye chakra. His presence atop a pyramid is a masonic symbol ensconced on our dollar bill. The founding fathers, who were initiates of the Brotherhood of Light, embedded this symbol of divine vision and other sacred concepts in the foundational documents of the United States of America.

One day, I was reading a decree that invokes the presence of the Elohim Cyclopea,

> "Beloved Cyclopea thou beholder of perfection,
> Release to us thy divine direction;
> Clear the way from all debris,
> Hold the immaculate thought for me."

I had been working on difficult areas of my personal psychology and needed help. I decided to write a letter to Cyclopea, my first ever to an elohim, asking him to assist me in working through my issues. I also asked him for a "delivery confirmation" that he had received my letter.

The following night, I woke up to a clap of thunder in my inner being. Simultaneously, the words, "I AM the Elohim Cyclopea" resonated through me. What a delivery confirmation! Later in the day, I remembered that the seven mighty Elohim are the seven thunders mentioned in the Book of Revelation, and rejoiced at the correlation.

God is healing you now

During my third pregnancy, I started to have gall bladder attacks. These were excruciatingly painful, like a knife going through your middle, and they would last anywhere from twenty minutes to a couple of hours. I kept praying to weather these attacks so I wouldn't have to get an operation with an unborn child, but the pain was almost intolerable.

Six weeks after giving birth, I had one of the strongest attacks ever and rushed to the emergency room. The surgeon was called in to take out my gallbladder. I was extremely nervous about the operation, knowing a six-week old infant was depending on me, but had no choice.

When I woke up from the anesthesia, the pain was worse than anything I had ever gone through before. The attendant in the recovery room was giving me Fentanyl, which is eighty times stronger than morphine, in twenty-minute increments, as I went in and out of consciousness.

As soon as the injection wore off, I was in agony again. This continued for more than five hours, before I was wheeled back to my room on Demerol. Not only was my mid-section in pain, but my entire body, which had been inflated with carbon dioxide gas during the operation.

Back in my room, I turned on the television, hoping to find something spiritually uplifting. I stumbled upon a live broadcast of the televangelist Benny Hinn, who was conducting a healing service.

I wasn't paying much attention to the program, as sore and groggy as I was, when a nurse came in and told me I would have to sit up. Every part of me was screaming. As I held on to her for help, I yelped, "Oh, how my shoulders hurt!"

At that very moment, from the television set I heard Pastor Benny say, "Someone just said, 'My shoulders hurt.' God is healing you now." I couldn't believe my ears. Then I felt a rush of light coming over me. It was so comforting for God to reach out in such an obvious way, over the pain.

During the next few days, each time I relayed the story to someone, I felt the same healing energy come upon me. The love and the light of this miracle continued to strengthen me through a challenging recovery.

The sponsoring master

It is important to choose a sponsoring master to assist you. You do this by invoking that master's presence daily and by performing good works in his or her name.

This process is described in the book, *The Masters and the Path*, by C. W. Leadbeater. Once you have chosen the master and he or she has accepted you, first as a probationary student, then as an accepted chela, the master can help you more quickly balance your personal karma. He does this by giving you token karmas, thereby preparing you for greater world service and ultimately for your ascension.

As the story goes, the unascended master Babaji was sitting around a campfire in the Himalayas with his disciples. All of a sudden, Babaji picked up a hot coal and burned one of his disciples' shoulders. "How cruel," said the others. "Why would you do such a thing?"

"Would you have preferred that he had fallen in the fire and burned to death, as his karma dictated?" Babaji explained. Through token karmas, the master assists his students and delivers them from a worse fate.

For the longest time, I waffled on choosing a master. I didn't want to subject myself to the disciplines of one master when it seemed like I could fly from flower to flower, like a bee in search of honey.

It took me years to settle down, so to speak, and when

I did, I knew that El Morya was the master I needed to pick. I knew that El Morya would not indulge my human consciousness and that I would be in good hands.

After working with El Morya for a number of years, I felt drawn more strongly than ever to the heart of Jesus. The many qualms about Jesus I had wrestled with, stemming from my discomfort with orthodox interpretations of his life, had melted away. What was left was the all-consuming love of his sacred heart, calling me, and I am thankful to El Morya for preparing the way.

To find your sponsoring master, you can meditate on a picture of El Morya each day until his eyes become alive, while giving the following prayer:

"Beloved El Morya, I pledge to be the manifestation
of your gemstone, the result of your efforts,
the victory of your sponsorship,
that this dispensation shall come to fruition
through the I AM HE consciousness
of my brothers and sisters and me
as the incarnate representatives of the
Great White Brotherhood, as above so below."

By giving this prayer, you will find your master too.

Mercy's flame

There is a time when we must face our dark side and the demons that lurk inside the hidden recesses of our subconscious and unconscious mind. This is a great challenge. We have to squarely face the motivations of evil that erupt in us, though we would rather not admit to them in the first place.

Most people feel ashamed. We would rather ignore our selfishness, our greed, our egotism, our anger, our mean-spiritness, our desire to be "better" than others, our lust for self-annihilation, and the overt or covert control strategies that we orchestrate to have our way. We coat these negative ambitions with a layer of denial, sophistication or self-justification, and then pretend they just don't exist.

When we genuinely carry on with our spiritual work, our dark side eventually riles up and comes out of the shadow. The hatchdoor to the filthy, creepy basement opens and it is time to clean house.

The word "guru" means "dispeller of darkness." This is what the ascended masters and our own higher self will do for us if we will let them in.

Kuan Yin is the Goddess of Mercy, revered by many in Asia. I invoked her assistance when I was going through some of my most intense spiritual battles, caught between the "hound of Heaven" and the "hounds of hell." While I struggled on the edge of the abyss, I experienced her compassion. I understood that she would not leave me bereft.

Kuan Yin is a cosmic mother to all. Chinese mantras, like *Nahmo ee roo Kuan Yin* invite her presence with us.

Past lives

Even though it is true that as a personality, we have only lived once, our soul has lived through a parade of personalities over many lifetimes. When I first began studying the teachings of the ascended masters, I wanted to know all about these past lives. I was curious and the idea was exciting. Had I ever been anyone famous, I wondered?

After many years, God started to reveal to me different past lives and I would go look up the historical records. Each time, there was a direct correspondence with events and initiations going on in the present.

I soon found out that working with past lives is not a fun and fascinating game for the curious. When the record of a lifetime is revealed by the ascended masters, a lesson must be learned. Opening the record brings up the energy, the difficulties and the mistakes of that life, which have to be processed by the soul and the personality, as if they were from the current life.

Doing so can be quite burdensome. For this reason, God only opens the record when you are ready, so you can better understand your current condition. Then, you invoke God's forgiveness through the violet flame to repair the wrongs and to make amends, and you determine not to fall on the same stumbling stones again.

Once you become aware of a number of lifetimes, you can see repeating patterns, regardless of the historical period, gender or geographical area of those incarnations. Eventually you become aware that you are more than your current personality, and more than the sum personalities of past lives. You begin to see how enemies and loved ones cycle and recycle with you through the centuries and how life is, as Shakespeare said, only a stage.

Each new play, each new story, each new character you become is for soul edification, to move forward in the pursuit of a greater love, understanding, compassion and wholeness.

The older your soul, the more lifetimes you have had, the more you are ready to process your past lives with the help of the violet flame. Most people who are attracted to the teachings of the ascended masters are older souls, prepared at inner levels for this challenge.

The Legend of the Ancient of Days

I once heard Elizabeth Clare Prophet read the story of Sanat Kumara and the 144 thousand. These beings of light came to Earth from Venus, a planet that is evolving in the etheric octave.

Even though our scientific equipment shows that Venus is inhospitable to life as we know it, there are many levels to life beyond what our scientific equipment can capture. Our mind may resist the idea that a great civilization is evolving on Venus in a higher dimensional frequency, but our soul remembers.

One day, sitting in meditation, a scene came to my mind's eye. I saw a group of men, women, children and angels, standing before Sanat Kumara and Lady Master Venus, connected by the deepest love and spiritual determination.

I described the scene to our friend, master painter Marius Michael George, and he illustrated it in brilliant colors. The scene became a poem, and later a book, now translated in a dozen languages. Line by line, I could feel the master Lanello's help, lending me the momentum he had garnered as Henry Wadsworth Longfellow in one of his past embodiments.

It is the story of many a soul:

> A long time ago
> On a star far away
> A council assembled
> In solemn array.

The question weighed heavy
On everyone's mind,
Was the future of Earth,
What to do with mankind?

The planet was burdened
With discord and strife
Human beings had forgotten
The purpose of life.

They had even begun
To walk down on all fours
In their eyes and their souls
God's great light shone no more.

"Earth must be dissolved,"
The cosmic council decreed,
"Her energy sent back
To the great primal sea."

I, Sanat Kumara
Arose from my chair
And invoked Opportunity
From those who were there:

"Let us give them a chance
And perhaps over time
These ones will remember
They once were divine.

"I will show them the way
I will be the front line
I'll bring mercy to Terra
If you would change your mind."

"My Son," said an elder,
"You know the law well:
You will be tied to Terra
Until your ranks swell.

"To win back her people
The flame in your heart
Must inspire them to love
And become Freedom's Star.

"These are new beginnings
For children of man
By your grace we do grant them
A fresh divine plan."

I gratefully knelt
Before the Great White Throne
Where the Nameless One blessed me
As I left for home.

"My son, they will call you
The Ancient of Days
To the Great Spirit in you
Give glory and praise.

"You are known throughout cosmos
For your eternal youth
May your Word now spring forth
Like a fountain of truth.

"I anoint you with Spirit
The I AM THAT I AM,
The ark of the covenant
And the embodied Lamb."

On my shoulders descended
A mantle of light
Power, glory and honor
Love, wisdom and might.

I bid the council adieu
And returned to my star
Where fair Venus awaited
With Holy Kumaras.

Winged messengers had announced
The cosmic council's decision:
That Earth was now granted
A new dispensation.

Our daughter Meta greeted
Me home with a kiss.
"Father, we're thankful," she said,
"For your courage and faith."

Though we rejoiced that night
In a grand ball reception,
Our hearts were weighed down
By a feeling of sadness.

The pain of separation
Could not be eclipsed
As we thought of the loved ones
We most surely would miss.

Many aeons would pass
Before we'd meet again
Our mission accomplished
Our victory at hand.

Twilight dropped upon us
A blanket of peace,
Our twin star twinkled softly
With ethereal surcease.

Then I looked to the mountains
And to my surprise,
Mine eye caught a spiral
Of light hovering nigh.

T'was the souls of my children
One hundred forty-four thousand
Fast approaching our palace
With joyful compassion.

The anthem of brotherhood
That echoed below
Still rings clear through these valleys:
Solstice Ode to Joy.

They reached for our balcony,
Stopped, lifted their eyes,
Then stepped forth to address me
'Neath violet skies.

I saw in their leader
My beloved son
Whose loyal steadfastness
Was rivaled by none.

"Our Father," he said,
"We have heard of your plight.
We will not let you down,
We will fight the good fight.

"We will prepare the way
We will help tend the flame
We will spread love and light
We will speak in your name.

"We will be at your side
When you enter the fray;
We will go first to Earth,
To keep evil at bay."

Their love was so touching
Their service so rare
I was moved beyond words
By their life-giving prayer.

These hundred forty-four
Thousand, my lady and I
Wept together for joy;
Angel legions stood by.

Then I called from among them
An hundred forty-four
To become our forerunners
In this epic untold.

The veil was now drawn
The heaven-world left behind
Clothed in bodies of flesh
They were born of mankind.

Neither castle nor palace
Would be their Earth home
Rather shacks, caves and huts
Humble hearths carved of stone.

They waxed strong and matured
In the ways of their kin
Yet their souls often stirred,
With an urge to transcend.

T'was a deep inner memory
That could not be erased
A magnificent city
That would now be their fate.

Came a day they set forth,
Friends and family behind,
To sail for blue horizons
And to seek holy ground.

Hearts brimming with passion,
Pressing on day and night,
Only intuition would guide them
Toward their appointed site.

From four corners of Earth
These great pilgrims arrived
Mighty warriors of spirit
Crossing lands, seas and skies.

The Gobi Sea was the place
Destiny had assigned
For these men to accomplish
Their purpose sublime.

When the pilgrims had reached
The final destination
One among them came forward
To express a shared vision:

"A resplendent white city
Is ours to erect
Reminiscent of Venus 'n
Divine architects.

"On a lush, verdant island
Seven temples our feat
Focusing sacred fire
In alabaster retreats.

"A beautiful bridge
Will be our first task
Over sapphire blue waters
Where others can pass.

"Fashioned with pure white marble
Engrained with finest gold,
Lined with sweet cherubs carved
Mem'ries of days of old."

By the sweat of their brow
Initiating the task
They hauled rocks, stones and metal;
Nine hundred years passed.

Down from neighboring hills
Savage hordes would attack
To destroy what was built
Cosmic goal now set back.

Determined and constant
The pilgrims kept their pace
Lifting up from the rubble
Planting trees in its place.

At the top of the island
The main temple was raised
Where Sanat Kumara's
Blessed feet one day would graze.

Twelve marble steps
Leading up to the throne
That was framed with perfection
By a high gilded dome.

A massive gold door
Shimmering rays in the sun
Like a gigantic mirror
To welcome each one.

Tall trees lined the path
Leading up to the gate
Reflecting pools, rainbow fountains
Vibrant floral parquets.

A sacred space was created
Where brotherhood shone
The builders called it Shamballa
To remind them of home.

The task was completed
The altars were groomed
With delicate flowers
Picked from most fragrant blooms.

Sanat Kumara would come now
For time had run short.
To depart unto Earth
With his devoted court.

He kissed his lady farewell
In a poignant embrace
And ascended o'er Hesperus
Into stellar space.

The souls that convened
Offered sweet hymns of praise
And he blessed them sincerely
With an affectionate gaze.

Then to their amazement
Midst a brilliant light trail
He vanished away
Like a comet's vast tail.

In Shamballa the builders
Waited with bated breath
For their lord to appear
As the prophecy said.

The birds hushed their singing
The seas ceased their sway
And all nature grew silent
On this momentous day.

Slow and majestic
His feet touched the ground
Then all life felt his presence
Though there was not a sound.

Fresh peace, hope and comfort
Each troubled soul stilled
As his Great Spirit swept
Over woods, lakes and hills.

Withered flowers that drooped
With new strength raised their heads,
And the laughter of children
Was heard once again.

The builders were happy
They wearied no more
And knelt in Thanksgiving
To honor their Lord.

Then upon the altar
The Ancient of Days
With a powerful fiat
Invoked a dazzling flame.

Threefold and immortal,
Pink, Yellow and Blue
Fount of love, wisdom, power
Precious life renewed.

From each flickering plume
Flashed forth filigree threads
To connect each one's heart
In a mystical web.

The crisis was over
The planet sustained,
And the Earth was redeemed
For a new golden age.

Now the end of this story
Is yours to create
As you search in your soul
For the keys it contains.

Close your eyes, try to see
Your mighty threefold flame
Anchored deep in your heart
'Tis your spiritual claim.

Pulsating, blazing
It waxes and spins
Helping you find your mission
So you too can ascend.

A song for our king

On New Year's Eve 2007, some friends had gathered in our home for a service and festivities. After cleaning the house, preparing food and tending to the children all day, I had become tired and discouraged. "I wonder whether there is any point in this," I thought.

The service was beautiful, and after ushering in the New Year, we all went to bed. Once my body was asleep, I was ushered consecutively by three masters into the presence of Sanat Kumara. His presence was surprisingly familiar and comfortable, like meeting up with an old friend, and I was exceedingly happy.

Sanat Kumara was dressed as a young king, in garments of ruby and pink silk, embroidered with gold. I remember standing next to him, and reaching out to hug him with my arm around his waist. "Not yet," he replied, with a twinkle in his eyes. I likened it to when Mary Magdalene had wanted to touch Jesus in his resurrected body and the master had said, "Do not touch me." Then Sanat Kumara asked me and my friend, Antonia, who had been at our service, to sing a song for him.

The next day, I told Antonia about the dream. She replied, "When I came into your home yesterday, there was a song playing. I so much wanted to sing it with you as a duet."

I looked up the words to the song she had heard. It was

a song about bringing in the New Year, and described some of my dream!

> "Good health, love and peace be all here in this place
> By your leave we will sing, concerning our King.
> Our King is well-dressed in silks of the best
> In ribbons so rare no king can compare.
>
> We have traveled many miles over hedges and stiles,
> In search of our King unto you we bring.
> Old Christmas is past, twelve tide is the last
> And we bid you adieu, great joy to the new."

The following day, I was driving my children home from school, still thinking about Sanat Kumara, when all of a sudden, a magnificent bald eagle shot straight up above our car.

The bald eagle is a sacred symbol of Sanat Kumara and the highest spiritual omen in Native American lore. This eagle rose in a straight vertical line above us. Under its wings, a number of small birds rose with it, protected by its wingspan, like the Divine Mother who rises into heaven with her children at her side.

A third-eye blessing

When I first found out that Elizabeth Clare Prophet was suffering from a physical affliction and would have to "retire," I cried. I knew I would miss her and the contact we were used to having with her.

However, since Mother's retirement, I can attest to her presence on inner planes, not only in my personal life but in the lives of so many of her students. We interact at night in the etheric planes and find a renewed sense of joy, understanding and purpose.

On one such occasion, there were many students standing in a large chapel. Some were at the front by the altar, and others, including myself, were sitting closer to the back. All of a sudden, Mother came in through the back door and asked us to line up for a blessing.

The people who were in the front were oblivious to what was happening right behind them. It was eye-opening for me to see that you could be in the same room and, depending on what your consciousness was dialing up, tune into two completely different events happening simultaneously.

When my turn came to receive the blessing, Mother placed her hand over my third eye. I experienced a healing. Mother took from me something that needed to go. Then upon awakening, I could still feel the light upon my forehead.

A rose from heaven

After eight years of marriage and three children, Brian and I were still living in an apartment in town. Our business had had a lot of ups and downs, and with the steep hike in local real estate prices, owning a home seemed completely out of reach. Each day I prayed for our home to manifest, but no response seemed forthcoming. We had to be patient.

One night, I went to the movie theater where "Therese" was playing, a movie on the life of Saint Therese of Lisieux. When the doors opened after the movie, we were greeted by a group of young catholics carrying buckets of roses. They handed each moviegoer a beautiful fresh rose. Attached to the rose was a picture of Saint Therese and on the back was an invitation to do the following novena to her, invoking a miracle.

> "Saint Therese, the little flower, please pick me a rose from the heavenly garden and send it to me with a message of love. Ask God to grant me the favor I thee implore and tell him I will love him each day more and more."

The card said to give this prayer, with five "Our Father's," five "Hail Mary's," and five "Glory Be to the Father's" for five consecutive days, before eleven o'clock in morning.

Then on the fifth day, it said to give the sequence twice. I wanted to ask her for a home for our family, but I was a little reluctant about whether or not this would work.

Still, I had nothing to lose. Saint Therese had been my patron saint since I was a little girl, and I remembered the walls of her church in Paris, covered with crutches and other objects that witnessed to her miraculous intercession.

I followed the instructions on the card. The day after I finished the novena, I drove right above the land where our house is now located. I called our friends Orlando and Antonia, who owned the land. Orlando told us he had subdivided the land and would give it to us. This set many wheels in motion.

I could feel Saint Therese's steely determination. As God said to Abraham, "Is anything too hard for the Lord?" Day after day, week after week, month after month, her personal sponsorship and investment, and her guiding hand were with us. Everything started to come together in spite of the most difficult odds and challenges.

Our initial construction lender went out of business. The foundation was mispoured by a contractor. A fraudulent team of builders stole more than $8,000 from us when finances were extremely tight, and delayed us for two months. The home structures arrived badly damaged because of horrible winds and the insurance would not cover the claims. There were also legal complications on the land that needed to be resolved. We were homeless for two months in the coldest winter with a newborn baby, and the day we absolutely had to move in was thirty below zero.

None of these setbacks deterred Saint Therese and her strength kept us plowing through every detail. At each turn was an equivalent or greater blessing, and with perseverance and faith, the obstacles started yielding to us.

Our loans were approved in time and we were able to manage the construction interest. Workers came to help and the damages were fixed. The land negotiations were finally resolved. We saved money in unexpected ways that more than made up for our losses. Friends offered to give us shelter when we no longer had a place to live. We received a full house of furnishings from the estate of Maria Scoble, a dear friend who had just passed away. And then when it came time for landscaping, an unexpected check arrived from the estate of my maternal grandmother.

Saint Therese's card is on my kitchen cabinet. Each time I look around me, I give thanks to the Father for this rose from the heavenly garden. Our home truly stands as a miracle and I know that if Saint Therese could do this for us, she can do anything of good for those who ask.

Windows of opportunity

While we were in the middle of our home construction, we took a weekend off to participate in a Worldwide Ashram prayer vigil dedicated to the master Morya. Our money was very tight, but we went ahead and gave a donation to the group. I was wondering how everything would work out and I heard El Morya within my inner being, telling me we would be well compensated.

When we got home, I was prompted to search the web for more construction information. I came upon a brand new site which listed our new home at $24,000 less than what was in our contract. The next day I called up the company that we were working with and they agreed to match the lower price. In one night, we had saved $24,000! A couple of weeks later, when I checked both sites again, I noticed the price of our home had gone back up to the original amount.

On another occasion, I wanted to take a family vacation but we were short by $1000. I was working on a publishing project that I knew was important to the masters, and I had volunteered a lot of extra time. I had also been looking at airfares for weeks. The night I completed the work, I thought to check the fares again. My higher self gave me exactly what dates to type in and the fares had dropped dramatically, enough to save us the thousand dollars!

I booked the tickets immediately and a few minutes later,

while our transaction was still processing, I noticed the advertised fares had already gone back up. In this small window of opportunity, God provided the money we were missing and blessed us.

Holy water!

Our construction was already underway when it came time to drill a well. The cost of the well was an unknown factor that had me stressed out for months. Orlando's well was one of the deepest and most expensive in the area. If we were to run into the same terrain, we would completely blow our budget. Every time I prayed about the well, I got the sense not to worry but I was still extremely concerned.

"God," I said, "you know where the water is and I don't. Please show me and help me feel the light."

I started to walk the land and came upon a spot where I felt light on my crown chakra. The light was focused in a circle. I could clearly feel the circumference of the circle, about ten feet around, and the center point where the energy was strongest. My neighbor and I put a stake in the ground there.

I could not come out on the day of the drilling, so I asked Orlando to show the drillers the stake. I was at home praying for the best possible outcome.

About thirty minutes later, I received a phone call from the driller. "Lady," he said, "I don't know what you did but we found abundant water at less than 50 feet. This is the shallowest well we have ever drilled and you just saved yourself $10,000."

I put the phone down, elated. I was so grateful for this

divine manifestation and for the joy of co-creating with God. The savings on the water made it possible for us to buy a hot tub, a luxury I had secretly wished for but which, up to that point, would not have fit our budget.

The blue chandelier

Alex Reichardt, long-time student and biographer of Mark and Elizabeth Clare Prophet, told me that Mother always had a chandelier in her home as a focus of the star Sirius. Sirius is the spiritual center of our galaxy on the etheric plane. The masters call it the white fire, blue fire sun. If you look at Sirius on a cold winter's night down from Orion's belt, you will see that it flashes blue, yellow and pink light. These pulsing colors can be seen even more vividly with a pair of binoculars or with a telescope.

I thought about getting a chandelier for our new home, and about how special it would be to inherit one of Mother's. I knew this was unlikely, since Mother was retired and most of her personal belongings had already been sold or given away.

About the same time, our friend Maria Scoble passed away, and another friend Alberta, was helping to manage Maria's affairs. She called me to see if I wanted to purchase some of the items in Maria's home. Above the dining room table was a chandelier that had once belonged to Mother. The chandelier was not part of the estate sale, but Maria's son said we could have it if we replaced it with a more contemporary light.

A few weeks later, Mother's chandelier hung in our living room. Like Sirius, it is blue and white and sheds a gentle blue light. Each time I look at it, I think of Sirius and of God's love, answering even our unspoken prayers.

Come back, right away

Eight months after giving birth to my son, I became pregnant. Even though I felt complete with three children, I could tell a new soul was pressing to come in, so I had left things in God's hands.

Then six weeks into the pregnancy, I miscarried. The doctor on duty told me that I might get pregnant immediately which surprised me, since it had taken months with my previous miscarriage for my body to recoup.

In the days that followed, I could feel the presence of the soul still around so I told him, "If you are going to come, come back right away because the cycle will be ending soon."

I conceived the same night. Three weeks later, Brian and I were talking and he said that considering our age, we shouldn't have any more children. I told him I wanted to take a pregnancy test just in case. The pregnancy test was positive, to my delight, because the soul had immediately returned.

After a few weeks, my body started to bleed again so I went back for another ultrasound. This time, it was a false alarm. My womb was sealed tight and the baby had a heartbeat.

When I told the technician that I never had a menstrual cycle between both conceptions, he didn't think a child could come back so quickly. "Are you sure you didn't have twins and miscarry one?" he asked. I was sure and the ultrasounds confirmed it. The souls coming in want to be born.

Out-of-body experiences

Brian remembers many of the teachings he receives and most of the work that he does out of the body. I don't recall as well as he does. Oftentimes, my experiences come back as dreams that can be hard to interpret, but at least a couple of times, I clearly remember slipping back into my body.

The first time was right after I had my second miscarriage. As I was walking out of the emergency room, I met my friend Georgia crying in the entry way. Her teenage son had just been "jumped" by a couple of thugs outside the main mall and was in critical condition. He was being flown to Billings, Montana by helicopter, where there is a larger medical center.

I comforted Georgia as best as I could and made intense prayers while driving home. I begged God to spare this boy's life and all of his faculties.

Early the next morning, I became aware that I was in the boy's hospital room. I remember the way the room was laid out and I remember looking at his head all bandaged up. I somehow knew that he would be all right, which was a great relief. Then, my higher self told me to go home to answer the phone.

I slipped back into my body and found myself laying on my pillow, just as the phone started to ring. The whole sequence was amazing to me. Later, I called Georgia to see how her son was doing. I told her I believed he would be all right, and he did fully recover.

In the spring of 2008 when I was pregnant with my fourth child, I became conscious that I was floating around the house while my body was sleeping. There was something in the house that was toxic and had to be removed. I was trying to find it but couldn't quite focus. Then, all of a sudden, my consciousness zoomed in on a cleaning product that was sitting on the kitchen island.

When I woke up, I remembered the experience. I really liked this product as it did such a good job cleaning just about everything. It had no bad smell and did not irritate my skin so I figured I had just had a crazy dream. For a few days I continued using the product and each time, I could feel my higher self encouraging me to take the dream seriously.

Finally, I read the label. It listed 2-butoxy ethanol. I looked online and discovered that this colorless, odorless solvent used in cleaning products could cause a host of birth defects, simply through skin absorption. I immediately threw the bottles out.

This experience taught me how much our divine self will guide and protect us, if we will lend an open ear.

A mountain of garbage

A couple of months after we had moved to our new home, a bag of mail that needed to be sent out accidentally ended up in the garbage. Brian had just taken the garbage to the dumpsters, where it is collected by the county. As soon as he came back, I realized what had happened and drove to the dumpster to get the bag back. When I got to the dumpsters, the garbage attendant told me that a truck had picked up the garbage within the last half hour and was headed to the incinerator in Livingston, about thirty miles down the road.

It was an impossible task, but I knew the mail had to be saved. In it were important documents that could not be lost. I raced down the highway to Livingston and got to the garbage depot. I told the workers what had happened. They said the garbage was already on its way to the incinerator. I begged them for a way to find the items and they agreed to help.

We were dealing with a mountain of garbage from all of the dumpsters in the area and the only way to go through it was one bulldozer shovel at a time. We literally started to sift through tons of garbage. One of the workers gave me a pair of gloves so I could pick up anything that might look like our mail.

For the next couple of hours, we continued, bulldozer shovel after bulldozer shovel, until eventually, most of the mail was found.

Wading through this garbage, I knew that I was balancing a karmic record relating to the triage of bodies on the battlefield. I also understood that this was not unlike the process God goes through to preserve souls. God seeks to save the seemingly unsaveable, and every last vestige of good that can be, is redeemed.

I returned to the car, mail in hand. Only then did I notice the smell that lingered on my belongings. What a grace! The stench had been subdued the entire time I had to tread this mountain of garbage.

The great initiator

Maitreya is a bodhisatva known for his kindness and for his role as the "great initiator." There is a prophecy that in centuries to come, he and his students will walk the earth once more.

Maitreya was the initiating master in the Garden of Eden, as well as Jesus' sponsoring master. His symbol is the "lion" described by the Prophet Ezekiel and by the apostle John in the Book of Revelation.

One night as I lay sleeping, I became aware that I was overlooking a bridge on the west side of the banks of the Seine, the river that flows through the heart of Paris. The sun was shining in a most brilliant way. All of a sudden a great lion appeared in the sky with a roar and I felt such love in my soul. I believe this was Maitreya and I sense a deeper connection with him since that moment.

Like Aslan in the *Chronicles of Narnia*, Maitreya's love initiates our souls, strips us from worldly illusion and impels us forward to learn the deeper mysteries of the great law of sacrifice.

Initiations on the spiritual path are a solemn affair, and not to be taken lightly. I did not realize just how serious they were until I had the following experience.

I was having a heated discussion with Brian in my sleep. I was protesting some aspect of my relationship with God, wanting God to conform to my expectations, rather than the other way around. While this was going on, I could tell that my higher self was urging me to rise up in consciousness, to let go and let God, but I did not listen. Instead, I continued to complain, demanding that Brian let me "process" my qualms.

At that very moment, a curtain-like divider opened above where Brian and I were standing, and I saw a group of ascended masters consorting. They sent a message, searing in its impact: "I had just failed my initiation."

My soul sank with grief and a profound sense of longing for what might have been. It was a deep disappointment and I had no one to blame but myself, though I knew blame would get me nowhere.

"Why didn't you tell me this was an initiation?" I prayed. "I would have better behaved."

I already knew the answer. Even though I had earned the initiation and the masters had set up the circumstance, I did not pass and that outcome could not be swayed.

I stood there, my mind scrambling for what to do next, when the master Kuthumi, who was part of the group, sent down a message with great kindness. "All you have to do is remember," he said.

I woke up remembering the moment, the encounter, and the experience of my soul, which was far more real than anything we go through on this side of the veil. My heart was set with a new determination. I did not want to fail again. I made the call for another initiation, for the opportunity to be trained, and for my consciousness to be raised, that my soul might be set free.

Ancient mystic rites

In the winter of 2007, I was invited to participate in a five-day training sponsored by The Mystical Order of the Divine Presence. During the event, I suffered from flu-like symptoms and completely lost my hearing, so most of my training happened on the inner. I knew that this training was sponsored by the ascended master Lanello, as his presence was so tangible through the day and through the night.

I had brought with me a book by C. W. Leadbeater called *Ancient Mystic Rites* and read before going to sleep. A section called "The Egyptian Mysteries" describes the rites of initiation passed down from Atlantean times to the ancient Egyptians and, ultimately, to Freemasonry and Theosophy.

Many of these rites were part of the science founded by Hermes, known to the Egyptians as Thoth, a world teacher who, according to Leadbeater, came 40,000 years ago to teach that God is "the light that lighteth every man that cometh into the world." The rites are based on the four divine archetypes of Father, Son, Mother and Holy Spirit.

Further in the book, Leadbeater describes the sacred path of thirty-three degrees common to the Masons, the Brothers of the Rose Cross and the Ancient Scottish rite. In the first degree, the probationary student, following a bath or baptism, is given a shield and learns to engage in the science of the spoken word through the giving of mantras. In the second degree, the student receives the Mysteries of Serapis for self-controlled thought. In the third degree, the Mysteries of Osiris are disclosed through an experience of spiritual death and rebirth.

The degrees that follow the third degree are earned by ministering to others, by understanding that we are all one, by realizing that Christ dwells in man, by sublimating our emotions into love, and by working out our negative karma.

At this point in my reading I fell asleep. It was late and on the morrow, we would be receiving a blessing ordaining us for greater service to life. As my body lay sleeping, I noticed that I was in a dressing room outside a corridor leading to a gathering of church ministers. A minister opened the door of my dressing room. She said that she could see I had been Lanello's wife in a past life. "Yes," I replied, "and he was a good husband."

The minister told me to put on my robe and come to the gathering. I followed her down the corridor and went to a table in the back of the room. Other ministers had already gathered, dressed in robes of white. When I took my coat off, I was wearing a long dress in the fashion of Arthurian lore.

The dress was deep emerald green velour with gold trim and white satin sleeves. Around my shoulders was a velour cape that was royal electric blue with gold trim. I gasped because the robe was so different from the other robes and I did not want to call any attention to myself.

I noticed someone sitting across the table. I looked closer and recognized my mundane personality with all of its flaws. I observed this "self" as a separate person from the "self" dressed in these new robes, where my consciousness was attached, and felt both compassion and interest for my lesser self. I understood that I had been "born again" and given a new mantle. Then, I woke up with a jolt, right before dawn. I had only slept a few hours.

Wondering what this dream meant, I opened the book where I had left off. I started to read about the thirtieth degree of Masonic initiation, which is a degree of knighthood. The prevailing color of this degree is electric blue edged with gold, the colors of the cape I was wearing.

As the student, or hierophant, approaches the thirty-third degree, his aura contains the masculine presence of Osiris as a brilliant white light shot with gold, and the feminine presence of Isis as the manifestation of truth, which is emerald green. The dress I was wearing in the dream, under the cape, was emerald green and white, lined with gold.

Leadbeater explains that the actual degree is conferred at the level of the Angel of the Presence. Two great white angels flash down from the higher heavenly octaves into the etheric plane to bless the candidate. I put the book down, so excited about these inner mysteries. It was time to get ready for our outer ceremony, sealing the retreat.

We gathered in a circle around the officiating ministers. When it was my turn to receive the blessing, I felt a tremendous amount of spiritual light descend. All of a sudden, my consciousness flashed up to the level of the Angel of the Presence, which had never happened before, and I saw two angels placing a crown on the Angel of the Presence.

Now I understood the inner significance behind the emblem of the Mystical Order of the Divine Presence: a cape topped with a crown, enfolding a shield on which are etched the images of the Lion, the Man, the Calf and the Flying Eagle. I understood that all outer activities of the Brotherhood of Light follow the same initiatic sequence.

Sincere aspirants on the path to God, from the times of Lemuria, Atlantis, and Ancient Egypt unto today, are initiated in a self-transcending cycle that becomes a spiral staircase leading to heavenly planes of consciousness. The steps and tools for preparation have been passed down through all of the mystery schools, from Atlantis and Lemuria, from the Pharaohs and Pythagoras, from the Rosicrucians and Freemasons, down to modern-day activities like the Keepers of the Flame Fraternity and the Mystical Order of the Divine Presence.

One's involvement in any of these activities serves as an invitation for inner initiation by the ascended masters and heavenly hosts, whereby outer rituals become talismanic tools for this timeless inner process.

The power of the thirty-third degree, Leadbeater explains, flows mightily as glory, strength and sweetness for service to others, and is only intended for a life of constant humility, watchfulness and service. It gives students the opportunity to draw down the sublime glory of the inner initiation, conferred at the level of the Angel of the Presence.

This spiritual mantle, like all mantles bestowed, comes

with a caveat. You cannot rest upon your laurels. When service is neglected or when the mantle becomes misused, the spiritual links to that mantle atrophy and the powers contained therein remain dormant. Then, the conferring angels and spiritual sponsors associated with the mantle, Leadbeater warns, turn their glance away to others more worthy.

A daily prayer

Years ago, I learned a prayer that I try to give daily. It is a prayer that summons the presence of Sanat Kumara and the legions of the thirteen archangels. In this prayer, you can list anything that you want God to look after, both in your personal life and in the world at large. The spiritual action is powerful, effective, right to the point, and can be invoked in very little time. It goes like this:

"In the name of my Mighty I AM Presence and in the name of Brahman, the one supreme God, I call to the Ancient of Days, Sanat Kumara, and the legions of the thirteen archangels to take command of the youth everywhere, and all attacks upon the youth including drugs, alcohol, tobacco, pornography, and all misuses of music and of the sacred fire of the Divine Mother. Take command of child abuse, the consciousness of abortion, war, terrorism, and all engines of destruction and loss of freedom. Take command of our nation, our government and all nations of the earth. Take command of our economy, our money supply and our energy needs. Take command of the nations of the Middle East, China, Tibet, Taiwan, Russia, Africa, and North Korea. Take command of the environment and elemental life. Take command of the lightbearers and protect all right action everywhere. Take command of my health, my family and my supply.

(Here you can make more specific requests.)

Let this be done according to God's Will. Amen."

The presence actual

People seek union with God in all kinds of ways, based on what they are passionate about. Some want to unite with God through action. This is called "karma yoga" in the East. They look for God's presence in the outworking of events. They want to be instruments of God, to see the walls come tumbling down, like in the Battle of Jericho. When they have such experiences, they say, "I know God."

Others would unite with God through wisdom and knowledge, the path of "yana yoga." They revel in divine illumination, to be able to understand the complexity of how everything works and fits together, like Einstein in his "eureka" moment. They strive to say, "I think I understand God."

Then, there are those who unite through love, "bhakti yoga," who say "I feel God." Such ones experience the divine when they are wrapped in a swaddling garment of mystical union, of Holy Spirit essence.

Beyond these three pathways lies an even more beautiful potential in store for everyone. In our Golden Age Psychology classes, we call it the "presence actual."

The presence actual integrates and goes beyond all of these forms of yoga. It is a spark within us that is non-conceptual. Beyond the outworking of events, beyond the comprehension of a complex scenario, beyond the overwhelming epiphany of feeling, it longs to be discovered.

The presence actual awakens in us as we balance the expression of love, wisdom and power in our lives. It is a divine flame within the heart that spins with scintillating, opalescent, rainbows rays. We awaken to the full potential of God within us, and share the experience of the psalmist, who witnessed, "Ye are gods, all all of you are children of the Most High."

Do you hear the people sing?

One summer, when I was a young teen attending 4-H camp, a girl who had grown up with gypsies offered to read my life line. I lent her my hand and she said, "There is a 'Y' here. In your early twenties, you will be presented with a choice that will change the course of your life if you allow it." At the time, I had no idea what she was talking about. Looking back, I believe she was referring to this teaching. I found the ascended masters when I was twenty years old and never did look back.

There is no greater joy than to experience the presence of God and to become aware of the friendship, the closeness and the intercession of masters, angels and elemental nature spirits in your life. It's a little like watching a black and white movie, and all of a sudden the technicolor comes in. Everything takes on a new joy, a new depth, and a new significance. It reminds me of the passage in the Book of Revelation that says, "Behold, I make all things new."

The masters are like spiritual mentors to us. They want us to balance our karma as quickly as possible, and then move on to greater levels of service and connectivity with them. We may have to endure increasing challenges for a cycle, and learn to exercise patience with our unfolding initiations. A big part of the process is being responsible for the energy of God flowing through us, and using that energy to serve and bless others. With practice, this does become a joy all of its own, and we become freer, happier and more empowered.

The masters understand that life here is a challenge. Many of them did, after all, walk in "coats of skin" too. They remember the struggles so common to this plane. In the face of adversity, in the heaviness of the moment, they offer us their momentum of joy.

"A twinkle of mirth is needed on earth," said El Morya in a 1958 dictation given to Mark Prophet. He stressed the need for a happy, confident approach to any situation and told his students to call upon him for assistance.

The masters have a well-founded optimism. They know that with God all things are possible and that the light of God never fails. They seek to infuse that faith in us, because it is through our free will that we make it come true.

I woke up one morning remembering a song they were singing in the retreats. It was the chorus from "Les Miserables," and was about our spiritual overcoming.

> "Do you hear the people sing
> Lost in the valley of the night?
> It is the music of a people
> Who are climbing to the light.
> For the wretched of the earth
> There is a flame that never dies.
> Even the darkest night will end

And the sun will rise.
They will live again in freedom
In the garden of the Lord.
They will walk behind the plough-share,
They will put away the sword.
The chain will be broken
And all men will have their reward.
Will you join in our crusade?
Who will be strong and stand with me?
Somewhere beyond the barricade
Is there a world you long to see?
Do you hear the people sing?
Say, do you hear the distant drums?
It is the future that they bring
When tomorrow comes!"

This is a crusade. Elizabeth Clare Prophet called it a revolution in higher consciousness. It is not for the faint of heart, but the rewards, as a preacher once said in jest, are "out of this world."

God promised, "Withhold nothing from me and I will withhold nothing from thee." Once you make your determination to internalize and externalize the light, all else becomes added unto you, as Jesus explained. More and more miracles can take place in your life.

Shakespeare wrote, "There is a tide in the affairs of men, which taken at the flood, leads on to fortune; Omitted, all the voyage of their life is bound in shallows and in miseries." Here is our tide, our 'Y' in the road. Will we follow it to our ascension? Or will we stay on a merry-go-round of ups and downs, lifetime after lifetime?

I have never seen anyone describe the journey more beautifully than Kahlil Gibran. His words are recorded in *The Prophet*, a book that my mother gave to me for my fifteenth birthday. The more I study these words, the more vast is their implication. I leave them with you, that we might, by God's grace, pass every test with love too.

> "When love beckons to you, follow him,
> though his ways are hard and steep.
> And when his wings enfold you yield to him,
> though the sword hidden
> among his pinions may wound you.
> And when he speaks to you believe in him,
> though his voice may shatter your dreams
> as the north wind lays waste the garden.
>
> For even as love crowns you,
> so shall he crucify you.
> Even as he is for your growth,
> so is he for your pruning.
> Even as he ascends to your height and caresses
> your tenderest branches that quiver in the sun,
> so shall he descend to your roots and
> shake them in their clinging to the earth.

Like sheaves of corn he gathers you unto himself.
He threshes you to make you naked.
He sifts you to free you from your husks.
He grinds you to whiteness.
He kneads you until you are pliant;
and then he assigns you to his sacred fire,
that you may become sacred bread
for God's sacred feast.

All these things shall love do unto you
that you may know the secrets of your heart,
and in that knowledge
become a fragment of Life's heart.

But if in your fear you would seek only
love's peace and love's pleasure,
then it is better for you that you cover your nakedness
and pass out of love's threshing-floor,
into the seasonless world where you shall laugh,
but not all of your laughter, and weep,
but not all of your tears.

Love gives naught but itself
and takes naught but from itself.
Love possesses not nor would it be possessed;
for love is sufficient unto love.

When you love you should not say,
"God is in my heart,"
but rather, "I am in the heart of God."
And think not you can direct the course of love,
for love, if it finds you worthy, directs your course.
Love has no other desire but to fulfill itself.
But if you love and must needs have desires,
let these be your desires:

To melt and be like a running brook
that sings its melody to the night.
To know the pain of too much tenderness.
To be wounded by your own understanding of love;
and to bleed willingly and joyfully.
To wake at dawn with a winged heart and
give thanks for another day of loving;
to rest at the noon hour and meditate love's ecstasy;
to return home at eventide with gratitude;
and then to sleep with a prayer for the beloved
in your heart and a song of praise upon your lips.

A spiritual statement of purpose

Years ago, I wondered, "What is life about? Why I am here?" Now I know there is a way, there is a purpose, there is a greater self that we can become. We have a spiritual mission.

In the business world, companies go through a great deal of trouble to figure out their mission statement. What does our mission statement look like, as spiritual beings, and what could we tell others who still search for a meaning to life?

I offer you this statement of purpose. Test it, share it, then shout it from the roof tops!

We are emanations of God, endowed with free will. Divine energy continuously flows through us as the life force that animates what we think, feel, say and do. We are meant to use this energy to do good, so that God's light can expand through us exponentially, blessing the people we interact with and the activities we engage in. If we invest our allotment of daily energy into negative behaviors and outcomes, we end up sabotaging ourselves in the short and the long run.

We are supremely accountable to ourselves first. We will reap what we sow, either in this life or another. What we send out comes back to us multiplied, so that we might learn from our experimentation in the divine laboratory of life. This is the law of karma, from which no one escapes.

Day by day, we evolve on several planes simultaneously. There is the personality, the self we know best, through which we think, feel and act. There is also our soul, the ineffable, deeper part of us that has lived many lives. Our soul's destiny unfolds through our personality choices. When our life magnifies the divine energy that flows through us, our soul is earning her immortality. When instead, we dally with darkness, we jeopardize our soul's calling and potential. This is why we must strive to conquer the negative patterns we created, that have followed us lifetime after lifetime.

We have a higher self, who evolves in the heaven-world while we evolve on earth. Our higher self watches over us, encourages us and protect us, especially when we make the call and strive to do good. Our higher self is the presence of the Christ, the divine mediator between God and man.

We also have friends in the heaven-world. Many of them walked the earth at one time or another, and mastered the challenges of life here. Their souls became immortal through the ritual of the ascension. They would teach us to do likewise, and we can call to them for help. We meet up with them at night while our bodies sleep, when our souls journey to the etheric retreats of the heaven-world for training.

The more we balance our karma and serve life, the more we fulfill our divine calling. An incredibly helpful tool to balance karma is giving mantras and visualizations to the violet flame.

Then, our soul will at last reach the level of maturity in God to merge with our higher self, nevermore to descend into lower levels of evolution. Like the ascended masters who went before us, we will become immortal. After our last physical body dies, all of our past-life personalities will crystallize into a divine personality that retains the light-essence of each lifetime. We will be new ascended masters, graduates from earth's schoolroom, free to move on through the many levels of the heaven-world.

Spiritual resources

The following resources help us to accelerate spiritually, to nurture an eternal relationship with masters in the heaven-world, and to resolve our psychology.

www.ethericretreats.com
Journey to all of the etheric retreats of the heaven-world.

www.becomingchrist.com
Find many of the lost teachings of Christ and ways to further explore your life mission.

www.sanatkumara.info
Discover teachings on Sanat Kumara from spiritual traditions worldwide, read the initiations of the ruby ray, and order *The Legend of the Ancient of Days*.

www.markandmother.com
True miracle stories about Mark and Elizabeth Clare Prophet, as witnessed by their students.

www.innerfamilyarchetypes.com
Study the inner family archetypes, powerful tools for self-awareness based on the four personalities of divinity,

introduced in the book *Why We Do What We Do: Four Pathways to Your Authentic Self.*

www.goldenagepsychology.com
Join us in spiritual classes for self-awareness and psychological wholeness, that will further expound on the teachings presented in this book.

www.mothercaspari.com
Read about Mother Caspari's legacy and the spiritual foundation of the Montessori method.

www.cosmicportals.org
Listen to the Music of the Spheres that comes through the Messenger of Music, Dorothy Lee Fulton.

www.tsl.org
A wealth of teachings and dictations by Mark and Elizabeth Clare Prophet, along with information on the science of the spoken word, the Keepers of the Flame Fraternity and many other topics.

www.spiritualawarenessfellowship.org
Find out more about about the Mystical Order of the Divine Presence.

www.worldwideashram.org
Participate in El Morya's Worldwide Ashram with devotees worldwide.

www.lightworldwide.net
A monthly newsletter for lightbearers worldwide.

www.markandelizabethprophet.com
Order exceptional biographies of Mark and Elizabeth Clare Prophet written by Alex Reichardt.

www.saintgermainfoundation.org
Read three must-have books, *Unveiled Mysteries*, *The Magic Presence* and the *I AM Discourses*.

www.anandgholap.net
Explore a vast number of helpful theosophical teachings by clairvoyants C. W. Leadbeater and Annie Besant, published online, including the landmark book *The Masters and the Path*.

www.theosociety.org
Learn about important theosophical works, including *The Voice of the Silence* by H. P. Blavatzky and *Light on the Path*, by Mabel Collins.

www.geoffreyhodson.iinet.net.au
Teachings on the ascended masters brought forth by clairvoyant Geoffrey Hodson.

www.agniyoga.org
Books dictated by El Morya to Nicholas and Helena Roerich, along with a search engine.

www.prosveta.com
Teachings of Omraam Mikhael Aivanhov and his teacher Peter Deunov, who serve the Eastern branch of the Great White Brotherhood.

www.yogananda-srf.org
Books and teachings by Paramahansa Yogananda about eastern masters of the Great White Brotherhood, including the most wonderful *Autobiography of a Yogi*.

www.ascendedmaster.org
Ascended master teachings given through the Bridge to Freedom, including helpful compilations by Werner Shroeder, like *Man, His Origin, History and Destiny*.

newagebible.tripod.com/corinneheline.htm
Explore the works of Corinne Heline, who was a student of Mother Mary.

www.mariusfineart.com
Beautiful original artwork by Marius Michael George, featured in *The Legend of the Ancient of Days*.

www.roerich.org
An incredible collection of mystical paintings by Nicholas Roerich from the Nicholas Roerich Museum in New York.

www.missionsaintgermain.com
A blogging web site about the ascended master Saint Germain.

Other recommended books are *Dweller on Two Planets* by Philos the Tibetan, *Brother of the Third Degree* by Will L. Garver, *At the Feet of the Master* by Alcyone and *Resume of a Disciple* by Alberta Fredricksen.

If you enjoyed this book, please tell others about it, and send them to **www.miraclesandmasters.com**

Join other spiritual seekers in the pursuit of self-transcendence.

Please visit

www.lightworldwide.net

We look forward to staying in touch.
                With love, **Therese**

About the author

Therese Emmanuel Grey has authored and co-authored several groundbreaking books, including *Why We Do What We Do: Four Pathways to Your Authentic Self*, *The Psychology of Success: Finding Your Inner Blueprint* and *The Legend of the Ancient of Days*. She now lives with her husband, Brian, and four children in Paradise Valley, Montana, and helps to facilitate personal growth workshops and retreats.

Printed in the United States
132126LV00004B/3/P